ZOLA

THE AUTOBIOGRAPHY OF ZOLA BUDD

ZOLA

Zola Budd with Hugh Eley

PARTRIDGE PRESS

LONDON · NEW YORK · TORONTO · SYDNEY · AUCKLAND

The publishers have made every attempt to contact the owners of the photographs appearing in this book. In the few instances where they have been unsuccessful they invite the copyright holders to contact them direct.

All-Sport: pp 5 *bottom right*, 6 *top left*.
All-Sport/Tony Duffy: p 8 *top right*.
All-Sport/Bob Martin: pp 5 *bottom left*, 6 *top right*, 11 *bottom left*, 10 *bottom*.
All-Sport/Mike Powell: p 9 *bottom*.
All-Sport/Dan Smith: p11 *bottom right*.
All-Sport/Rick Stewart: p7.
Associated Press Ltd: pp 6 *bottom*, 8 *top left*, 8 *bottom*.
Quintus Budd: pp 15 *bottom*, 16.
Charles Corbett: p 15 *top*.
Daily Mail: p 5 *top*.
Hoffie Hofmeister: p 4.
Hannes Pieterse: pp 12 *top*, 13.
The Press Association Ltd: p 11 *top*.
Colin Urquhart: p 3 *bottom*.

TRANSWORLD PUBLISHERS LTD
61-63 Uxbridge Road, London W5 5SA
TRANSWORLD PUBLISHERS (AUSTRALIA) PTY LTD
15-23 Helles Avenue, Moorebank, NSW 2170
TRANSWORLD PUBLISHERS (NZ) LTD
Cnr Moselle and Waipareira Aves,
Henderson, Auckland

Published 1989 by Partridge Press
a division of Transworld Publishers Ltd
Copyright © Zola Budd 1989

British Library Cataloguing in Publication Data
Budd, Zola, 1966–
Zola: the autobiography of Zola Budd.
1. Athletics. Running. Budd, Zola Biographies
I. Title II. Eley, Hugh
796.4'26'0924

ISBN 1-85225-089-5

Printed in Great Britain
by Mackays of Chatham plc, Chatham, Kent

Contents

'We are children of our landscapes;
it dictates behaviour and even thought
in the measure we are responsive to it.'

from *The Alexandria Quartet* by Lawrence Durrell

1

Aboard the Buddwagon

When I heard on 6 April 1984 that I had been granted British citizenship, it should have been the greatest moment of my life. But there was no rush of adrenalin, no relief that I finally had the chance to run internationally after competing in the vacuum of South African athletics against the same faces every week. Instead, I saw the passport that thrust me into the world spotlight as a symbol of my abuse. All I had ever wanted to do was run. Although I was just seventeen, running had become a way of life for me. It was something special, something to cherish. I ran because I loved it and because it made me feel good, but from the moment I became a British citizen I felt that I had become a commodity and that my life would never again be the same.

Shy, impressionable and easily influenced, I was bewildered by the controversy generated by what opponents of South Africa's racial policy saw as a passport of convenience, and I was firmly under the control of my father, Frank, and coach, Pieter Labuschagne. They had helped put me on top of the world, but they never stopped to consider my feelings when they decided I should go for gold at the Los Angeles Olympic Games. Their attitude changed after I broke Mary Decker's world 5,000 metres

1

record in Stellenbosch on 4 January 1984, when, running barefoot, I clocked 15:01.83. It seemed to me that Daddy and Pieter realized then that they could advance their own careers as well as my own. Daddy recognized my commercial value, while Pieter was already savouring the prestige he would get as the coach of a world class athlete able to compete outside the confines of a country ostracized because of its apartheid policy. Together with the *Daily Mail*, which arranged the cloak-and-dagger operation to get me to England in what was, for it, a massive and highly successful publicity stunt, they turned me into some kind of circus animal. I was expected to perform, and perform well, every time I put a foot on the track.

This was in total contrast to my career in South Africa, where winning wasn't everything. There, I had some semblance of control over my life, but that disappeared when I was plucked away from everything I loved and put in an environment where I, as a person, no longer counted. The travel document that gave me entry to international athletics had become the passport to fame and fortune for my father and coach.

I felt I was harshly exploited by the *Mail*, which paid a bargain basement £100,000 for exclusivity of my 'story'. I found its whole campaign was so exaggerated, such a façade. At seventeen and coming from an Afrikaans background, I could not even express myself fluently in English, let alone handle a press conference. Home for me was with my family in the Free State, surrounded by animals, yet, at the stroke of a pen, I suddenly underwent a traumatic nationality change. It was farcical for the *Mail* to portray as British a young girl from a smallholding near Bloemfontein. I was forced into an artificial world totally alien to me and expected to act normally, churning out world class running times as the *Mail* squeezed from me every drop of publicity it could to boost its circulation. I tired quickly of the countless contrived photographs and still remember vividly one session at the zoo where, after

2

posing in front of all the animals, I felt like one of the monkeys instead of Britain's hope for the 3,000 metres gold medal in Los Angeles.

The *Mail* went to extraordinary lengths to justify its role in bringing me to England and I shall never forget the irony of the statement made by editor Sir David English. 'The *Daily Mail*', he said, 'firmly believes that Zola Budd will become a great British athlete. This is why we have helped her and her family to come to this country so that she can run for Britain – the country she wants to represent in world athletics. As a British citizen she will be able to run against international competition and we felt it would be a tragedy if she had to run for any other country when her heart lies here.'

It was news to me that my heart lay in Britain. At the time I was desperately unhappy in England and even telephoned my coach shortly after my arrival to tell him that I didn't want to go to the Olympics. Pieter said 'fine', but my father and the *Mail* had other ideas. I had the impression that Daddy was not going to let £100,000 slip through his fingers and the *Mail* was desperate to protect its 'investment'.

When my father first suggested running internationally, I jumped at the chance. I was, at the time, the fastest woman on earth over 5,000 metres, beating Mary Decker's time by 6.45 seconds, and the prospect of taking on the world excited me. Initially, I only looked at the short term, the Olympic Games, but with me being so naive at that stage my father should have known better.

Under Daddy's dominance I wasn't yet able to make my own decisions, and I couldn't stand being a symbol for the *Mail*. I felt like a page three girl in the *Sun* and I was very unhappy that my *Mail* contract antagonized other journalists who, instead of getting exclusive interviews with what they regarded as the hottest property in the country, had to settle for quotes from me at press conferences, where the men from the *Mail* were always on hand to make sure I didn't say too much.

Even worse, Daddy took the lion's share of the *Mail* money. Of the original £100,000, £20,000 went into my British trust fund, Pieter got £20,000 and my sisters Estelle and Cara and my brother Quintus, Cara's twin, received £5,000 apiece. That left £45,000 with Daddy . . . and I have never seen a penny of it. When I asked him about it, Daddy said the money had been used for 'expenses', but I found that strange because the *Mail* paid for almost everything when we were in England before the Games, including our accommodation.

My father's attitude was indicative of what was to come as everybody jumped on the Budd bandwagon. Already a high-profile athlete because of the controversy over my selection for Britain at the Olympics, the tangle with Mary Decker added fuel to the flames. I was a saleable commodity and I believe I was exploited; I was vulnerable; frightened and confused, the focus of media men around the world and an easy target for the anti-apartheid lobby.

When I finally realized that Daddy only saw dollars when he looked at me – a feeling that was reinforced when I learnt that during negotiations for my contract with Brooks shoes, Daddy planned to act as my agent and take as a fee thirty-five per cent of everything I earned. Luckily for me John Bryant put a stop to that, but my father's general attitude to me became intolerable and I was to walk out of the house and move in with Pieter and his wife, Carin, in Guildford. At seventeen, I had already become the centre of a power struggle between Daddy and Pieter and I turned my back on my father just two weeks before the Olympics. I doubt that the rift between us will ever completely heal.

My mother, Tossie, and my father were later to divorce. They had not got on well ever since I can remember, but at the time I blamed my athletics for their separation and it felt as though the bottom had fallen out of my world. In desperation I turned to Pieter, but, like so many other

4

relationships in my short career this one would eventually turn sour. Pieter is a good coach, one of the best, but even he did not really understand what motivated me once I had got to the top. After Mary's fateful fall at Los Angeles I just wanted to get back home – to my real home, Bloemfontein, where I could be happy – but Pieter could not bear the thought of losing me. For some strange reason, nor could Jannie Momberg, a wealthy Cape wine-farmer and politician who backed independent candidate and former South African ambassador Denis Worral in the 1988 South African general election.

I still don't know why Jannie, a vice-president of the South African Amateur Athletic Association, was so willing to become involved in my career. He wanted only what was best for me and he gave me a great deal of help when I needed it. All I could give in return was achievement on the track and cross-country course, but perhaps that was enough for a man with a deep love of the sport: to see the athlete he had helped back into international competition reach the very top. Jannie was thrilled when I won the world cross-country championship, as was his associate, Cape industrialist and wine-farmer Graham Boonzaier, who gave me the financial backing I needed to get back into international athletics after the débâcle in Los Angeles.

Those three, Pieter, Jannie and Graham, can certainly take the credit for my return to England after the intervention of Mel Batty, from the Brooks shoe company and *Mail* man John Bryant, who came to South Africa on a 'Save Zola' campaign after the Olympics. But Pieter was a changed man. Winning became everything to him, and he put a lot of pressure on me when I did not perform to his high expectations. He was determined that I remain 'British' and while realizing that it was essential for me to train in South Africa before I raced overseas – something I still believe I had every right to do – he discouraged me from spending as much time with my family as I would have liked.

Lots of British athletes train in the United States to

5

escape the worst of the weather; and I too have always been very aware of my environment. Without the sun on my back and the familiar smells of the Free State veld, I just could not function properly. I found it difficult to train effectively in England's cold, wet climate, yet even when I returned to South Africa, I didn't have much opportunity to visit my family in Bloemfontein. This was in spite of the fact that like any young woman who had been away from home, I needed to be with my mother, brother and sisters, at least for a week or two, because I missed them terribly.

If, when I was feeling low and not training well I told Pieter I wanted to go home for a while, he would reply: 'You will be nothing if you don't win. If you don't keep running, you will end up as a nobody, living on a smallholding with your mother.'

That hurt; it hurt a lot, because my mother had done nothing but give me love and encouragement; she is a wonderful person who has had a hard life. She was seldom happy with my father, and when I started showing signs of becoming a world-class athlete Daddy virtually cut her out of his life. She became an object, a 'middel tot 'n doel' as we say in Afrikaans, and I can never forgive Pieter for trying to use Ma's situation as a typical South African housewife as a way of making me continue running.

This was one of the main reasons for the final split between me and Pieter. Although he had done so much for me, I found it impossible to maintain a relationship with a coach who wanted me to brush aside what I felt were important aspects of my personal life in a quest for good performances. I make no excuses for staying with Pieter as long as I did even though I was often on an emotional merry-go-round. Without my father around, I came to rely on Pieter. He was, after all, the man who had first made me believe in myself. He had put me on the path that would eventually lead to the greatest moment of my life, winning the world cross-country championship in Portugal in 1985,

6

but once I started losing Pieter seemed to take it as a personal affront. My failure as an athlete became his failure as a coach.

Pieter didn't believe me when I told him in 1986 that I was injured, and became annoyed when I didn't train or run well. He was devastated when I was 'only' fourth in the 3,000 metres at the 1986 European championships and I was shocked when he asked afterwards how he was going to explain my poor showing to people in South Africa. In the end we parted after a meeting in Stellenbosch, when British athletics promoter Andy Norman said it would be better for me to have a British coach – he suggested Harry Wilson – instead of a South African.

I have constantly been criticized for my dependence on other people, but having grown up in a tight-knit family, I found it difficult to function without a father-figure. Although there was always friction between my English-speaking father and my Afrikaans mother, I was very close to Daddy until my athletics career began taking off. When I turned my back on him, I faced a void that had to be filled and that's why I relied on people like Jannie and Pieter. Jannie was determined that I should make the best possible use of my opportunity to run for Britain and he did all he could to help me realize my potential. He played a pivotal role in my success and when I was winning he was always there for me, but at the end of 1986 and in early 1987, when my injury began taking its toll on my performances, I started losing contact with him as he slowly drifted out of my life. I heard from Jannie less and less and our relationship ended in July 1987 after I met Fanie van Zijl.

It was Fanie who introduced me to Dr Ron Holder, the applied kinesiologist who was to cure my hamstring injury with his use of orthotics, or wedges, in my running shoes. I will always be grateful to Fanie for that, because Dr Holder had a profound influence on my life as he introduced me to literature and classical music and showed me that there was more, much more, to life than just athletics. But while the doctor helped me over my injury and then became my friend, pressure of business put Fanie out of reach just when I needed him most.

With the knowledge of British Amateur Athletic Board officials, Fanie became my real coach, while John Bryant acted as a 'front'. It was through my association with Fanie that I attended the cross-country meeting in Brakpan and New Year's Eve race in Randfontein – the two incidents the International Amateur Athletic Federation used to recommend my suspension for twelve months; but when the chips were down and I was fighting for my international survival, it felt as though Fanie had left me in the lurch. 'Go to the beach', was his advice to Dr Holder when we telephoned Fanie from America to ask him what to do when the IAAF ruled in March 1988 that I was ineligible to run a 10 kilometres race in Central Park pending an inquiry into my status.

When the IAAF voted unanimously on 16 April 1988 that the BAAB 'ought to consider a suspension of the athlete from international athletics of at least twleve months' for 'being in breach of the spirit of the rules of the IAAF', I was near breaking point. I was tired of being a political football to be kicked around by the IAAF and all the others who thought that by punishing me they would be striking a blow against South Africa. Apart from my family and Dr Holder, there seemed to be nobody on whom I could rely for advice. When I was on top of the IAAF's hit list I had to face the music alone and when eventually the pressure became unbearable I found sanctuary in South Africa. It was only then, at the age of twenty-one, that I became the mistress of my own destiny. It had taken time for me to grow up, to mature and stand on my own two feet, but I finally had control over my life. Although my exclusion from the 1986 Commonwealth Games and 1988 Olympic Games still hurt, I was able to look ahead and dream about the day I would be re-admitted to world athletics. An athlete first and foremost, I had initially been reluctant to enter the

8

world arena, but, once there, I realized that that was where I belonged. Running for Britain was my birthright and I would do everything possible to continue my career.

This is the story of my climb to the top of the world and fall to the depths of despair.

2

Running from Death

I was born by emergency Caesarean section on 26 May 1966 at the National Hospital in Bloemfontein, and both my mother and I almost lost our lives. I weighed seven pounds and went straight into an incubator amid fears that I had suffered oxygen deprivation during the birth, while Ma was unconscious from loss of blood. My mother had to wait five days before the hospital staff allowed her to hold her sixth child in her arms, and she remembers me as being 'a tiny little thing'.

It says much for Ma's fortitude that she pulled through, but then she was no stranger to difficult births and tragedy. She had been dangerously ill after my sister, Estelle, was born and she had gone through the agony of nursing a son, called Frankie after my father, who was terminally ill. Later, she would lose another child, my sister Jenny, but each time fate dealt her a cruel blow she bounced back and devoted her life to the welfare of her remaining offspring.

Jenny came first, on 10 July 1955, followed by Estelle on 17 February 1957, Frankie on 1 March 1960, the twins, Cara and Quintus, on 28 September 1961 and then me.

Frankie was born with a liver disorder and my parents were faced with the terrible knowledge that, in spite of

10

the best medical help, he was unlikely to survive. He had several operations at the Johannesburg hospital, but Ma says that when she took Frankie home, she had prepared herself for the fact that his grip on life was tenuous and he died on New Year's Day in 1961.

Fears that I might be brain-damaged from lack of oxygen during birth were quickly dispelled and Ma says I made remarkable progress once I was out of the incubator. I walked at thirteen months and while I was a baby everybody made a tremendous fuss of me. I was blessed with a quick mind and could read before I went to school at the age of five. I could also run, and in my first year at Onze Rust primary school won the 60 metres race for my age group on the annual sports day.

My love for animals was passed on to me from my parents, both of whom preferred the wide-open spaces to city life. Although Daddy had a printing business in Bloemfontein, he found farm life irresistible and the family moved around a lot when I was small: from a smallholding to town and back to a smallholding.

Sadly, my parents did not enjoy a happy marriage and there was always tension in the house. I can't remember any real show of affection between Ma and my often moody father and, although my parents were always there when I needed them, they were often too busy earning a living to support a large family to be able to devote to each of us as much of their time as they might have liked. Daddy had the printing firm and the farm to look after, while Ma ran a catering business from home. I'm not saying they ignored us, far from it, but force of circumstance made the Budd children turn to each other for support and we became very tight-knit.

With my father being English and my mother Afrikaans, there was a culture clash in the home which may have contributed to the strain on their marriage. My paternal great-grandfather had fought for the English in the Boer War, while my maternal grandfather had been on the

11

opposite side. My father was liberal in his outlook on life, my mother conservative; he spoke English, she Afrikaans. They conversed in English and my brother and sisters spoke Afrikaans to Ma and English to Daddy. Although I could understand English, I spoke only Afrikaans when I was growing up, even to my father, and I only felt comfortable with English after the start of my international career.

Fortunately, the conflict between my parents did not rub off on to the children and we loved Ma and Daddy for what they were. As the youngest member of the family, I was spoilt and I had great fun growing up on a farm. Going to school was very exciting – I couldn't wait to wear a uniform just like my brothers and sisters – and the fondest memory I have of my father is his warm hand in mine after I won the 60 metres dash in my second year at school. It was the second year in a row I had won the sprint on sports day, although it was a painful experience! Instead of wool, there was a nylon cord across the finishing line, and it cut my neck, leaving a scar I carried around for several years. Daddy was there to cheer me on – until we parted company in 1984, he went out of his way to give me every opportunity to further my athletics career – and, pleased as Punch, he proudly walked with me to the teachers to tell them all about my victory.

Daddy was fanatical about poultry, and even in my teenage years I used to help him with the chickens. Daddy entered his best birds in agricultural shows, and one of my chores was to help him catch his show chickens. I became expert at preening them, washing their feet, cleaning their beaks and putting them into cages. It was fun feeding and watering the chickens every day and turning eggs in the incubator, gazing with wonder as a tiny beak chipped away at its protective shell. At the shows I would stalk around the exhibition hall with Daddy, carefully examining all the chickens and wondering if ours would win a prize.

My mother's fancy was ducks – there was always a duck pond at the smallholdings on which we lived – and, being a

12

child with a vivid imagination, I would spend hours next to the pond, holding earnest conversations with my feathered friends. Ma also collected stray lambs and there was never any shortage of animals with which I could occupy myself once I had finished my homework.

Farm life turned me into a real tomboy and I was the despair of my mother. Deeply tanned from hours spent in the sun and with my short hair streaked blonde, I wore tee-shirts and shorts and was nicknamed 'Boetie' by the neighbours and the people who ran the shops near the farm, because I looked like a boy. Getting me to wear a dress was almost impossible and, except on special social occasions, I only wore dresses when we went to church.

My best friend when the family moved to a smallholding at Bainsvlei was a black boy, Thipe. He was the son of one of the farm workers and we became inseparable. I couldn't wait to finish my homework every afternoon so that we could play together and those were some of the best times of my childhood. While the rest of South Africa saw each other as whites, blacks, coloureds and Asians, we were free of prejudice. We were friends who couldn't care less what colour we were – and what fun we had!

Pretending to be Tarzan in the veld was one of our favourite games, or we might make our own gardens. We fought, cried and laughed and roved every inch of the farm in search of excitement and pleasure. Thipe taught me how to split sunflower seeds with finger and thumb nails to eat the sweet kernels; we raided the fruit trees, looking for the first soft peaches or apricots of the season, and stole biscuits from the kitchen.

During winter we would hunt for dry wood and make fires in the evening, sometimes dancing around the flames in a wild ritual or else content to sit in the warmth, talking softly as we watched the sun set and savoured the acrid smell of the smoke. Sometimes Thipe would entrance me with tales from African folklore and scare me with stories about giant spiders that chased you around the veld.

13

In summer we would wait anxiously for the rain which was so important for Free State farmers. I was fascinated by the contrasts in the seasons and it was exhilarating to watch the clouds build up before a torrential downpour. In Africa you can actually smell the ground after the first few drops have fallen, and an additional treat was the fact that in the Budd household rainy weather was pancake weather. Ma traditionally made pancakes when it rained, so it was just as well we lived in South Africa and not England!

When we heard about something new, like karate, Thipe and I would immediately try it out ourselves, and we often got into trouble for making too much noise or being late for the evening meal. Hide-and-seek would keep us occupied for hours and I experienced the elation of racing when we had contests between ourselves and other children in the neighbourhood up and down the gravel roads on and around the farm.

Thipe and I were fortunate to live away from the city, because we had the opportunity to seek out and enjoy all the good things that nature provides. We would search for large, flying insects, tie threads to their legs and make them whizz around our heads like helicopters, or lie in wait for the bats that roosted in the roofs of the farm building and try vainly to hit them out of the air with long sticks. Not even a hole in the ground was ignored. If we found a pit or trench it instantly became a mine and unusual rocks and stones were gold and diamonds, scratched out of the earth and guarded jealously.

The animals, of course, took up a lot of our time, but a job like cleaning the duck pond invariably turned into a game. One of the ducks was short-tempered and we would tease her until, with much quacking and wild flapping of wings, she would come after us. There was only one tree nearby in which to seek refuge from her hard bill and it could only accommodate one child. When the duck came after us we had to race for the tree – and the person who came second got pecked!

I lost contact with Thipe when we moved back to town and my life was very empty without him. Ours was a simple friendship – the best kind. Neither of us could profit from the other, we didn't have possessions the other coveted and we were not bound by the laws of the land which precluded the free mixing of people from different racial groups. My relationship with Thipe taught me that the colour of a man's skin is not important and it saddens me to think that the lesson I learnt as a child is still ignored by so many South African politicians.

When I wasn't with the animals, with friends like Thipe, or helping around the house, I did a lot of reading. It was always a treat for me to go to town with my mother every Friday for the weekly shopping expedition and I saved my pocket money to buy books. My desire to learn from or amuse myself with books developed during my first year of school at Onze Rust. In an unsettled school life, I attended Onze Rust for two years and then spent a year at Jim Fouche junior school. When we moved again I went to Willem Postma primary and stayed there until I finished standard five.

With Ma running a catering business it was natural for me to be called in to help and one of my tasks was making the mayonnaise. There were buckets of the stuff in the house and I also became a dab hand at trifles and meatballs. That I had to wash up went without saying, and I served food and cleared tables at many of the functions where my mother provided the catering. It was hard work and on one evening I was so tired that a friend pushed me to and from the kitchen on a trolley!

I ran my first 'long distance' race at junior school when they introduced a three-lap event over 1,200 metres. This was something new, and, considering myself a sprinter, I had not even thought about taking part. But Daddy, with typical foresight, had other ideas. 'Come on Zola,' he said at our annual school meeting. 'Give it a go.' I was not, however, particularly enthusiastic – having just run the sprints

15

and the relay I was tired; but, urged on by my father, I took the great step into the unknown. Could I last three laps? No problem. I won by miles in the first indication that I would be best at the longer distances when I eventually started taking athletics seriously. At that stage it was just another school activity, but even then my father attended as many athletics meetings as possible to shout his encouragement.

It was my father, too, who gave me the first pet I could really call my own. I was eleven and we were living in town when Daddy came home one day with a small kitten whose tail had mysteriously been chopped off. I christened her Stompie and she was lovely, putting her paws on my shoulders when I first held her. It was love at first sight and I was thrilled because she was all mine. I lavished affection and attention on Stompie and regarded her as my friend and confidante. She was the patient when I played doctors and the student when I was the teacher.

I also became the proud owner of two large white rats. The pair became six, the six became twelve, and my mother said 'no more' in the face of such prolific breeding. I kept the female and, after carefully counting the rest, took them to the pet shop in a bucket to sell. A recount at the pet shop revealed that two baby rats were missing; they had escaped in the garage and spent the rest of their days living under the freezer. I was never able to catch them, but I did put food out regularly and I trusted to luck that they would survive when we moved.

Stompie, of course, had more than a casual interest in the rat I kept and I tried to make them friends. She wouldn't touch the rat when I was around, but I had to be quick if I fooled Stompie into thinking that I was not around by hiding. I also kept mice, but when they began to multiply they went the same way as the rats.

Instead of following Cara to the co-educational Dan Pienaar high school my father decided that 'Zola must become a lady'. To this end I was enrolled in the posh all-girls Oranje Meisies school. It was not a prospect I

16

relished, but Daddy obviously wanted the best for me, thinking, perhaps, that I would shed my tomboy image. 'It will be good for you,' he told me. 'The school has an excellent reputation.'

Oranje Meisies certainly had a good name and its pupils included many of the best young ladies in Bloemfontein. But that was the trouble. The pick of the crop all came from wealthy families and while the Budd family lived comfortably, I did not share the materialistic attitude of the girls I associated with in standard six. We came from different backgrounds, with me putting more value on life around me than on what I owned. To make matters worse, I was in the A grade with the brightest students, and everybody was very aware of their status. The children in the lower grades didn't like us much because we were the 'brains' and I felt I didn't fit in.

The class-consciousness rubbed off on me and I used to dread it every day when my mother came to pick me up from school in the old Volkswagen Kombi, or mini-bus, she drove to make her deliveries in the catering business. It was a real rattletrap – you could hear the gears squealing in protest before she came around the corner – and I felt terribly out of place climbing into the Kombi while the other girls were collected by doting parents who drove a BMW or Mercedes Benz.

I feel guilty when I recall my embarrassment. Ma worked hard and didn't have time to keep beautifully groomed like the other mothers. Working clothes were good enough for her and the Kombi was practical, even though it had a hole in the floor-boards and the passenger seat in the front had been removed to give her more space in which to pack all the food she cooked.

Even worse than the Kombi was an old green bakkie, or pick-up truck, which looked even more conspicuous when Ma parked it outside the school. I dreaded the days Ma drove the bakkie and I clambered into the cab as quickly as I could to avoid the eyes I was sure were following me.

17

But it was Ma who came to my rescue. Aware that I was unsettled at Oranje Meisies, she arranged for me to switch to Dan Pienaar and I only found out when she arrived at school one day with a Dan Pienaar uniform in the car. Was it for me? Yes. What a lovely surprise. I had not been happy at Oranje Meisies; my marks were bad and I started having bad dreams about the school. I didn't belong there and it didn't help when I had a foot operation to remove a small bone from my arches during my year at Oranje Meisies. The surgery was done during the holidays and with my feet in plaster, I was housebound and annoyed at having my freedom restricted by two plaster casts.

The big change in my life came in 1980, when I joined Cara at Dan Pienaar and met Pieter Labuschagne for the first time. He was a history teacher and the school athletics coach and he invited me to join his squad after some of the girls from Dan Pienaar, whom I had beaten the previous year, told him I had switched schools.

Like most South African pupils, I respected all my teachers and Pieter was no exception. He was somewhat reserved and I always thought of him as 'Meneer', the equivalent of the English 'Sir'. At first I wasn't especially taken with the idea of doing athletics seriously, but I started training every day and the improvement soon became apparent.

I trained through the summer of 1980, my athletics kit comprising two tee-shirts and one pair of shorts, and tasted success in my first season with Pieter when he introduced me to cross-country running. At first I hated it – in one race my friend Stephanie Gerber, who would become my great rival on the track, had finished and was in her tracksuit by the time I crossed the line – but I persevered and was duly rewarded. In July I won the South African Schools cross-country championship and in August I was second in the Free State under-14 championships. Both races were in Bloemfontein and I was selected to represent my province in the national junior championships in Pretoria on 30 August, where I came 12th behind Christine Bornman.

Of fleeting concern to me at the time was the fact that my sister Jenny, eleven years my senior at twenty-four, was about to go into hospital to have a lump in her arm removed. But what at first I thought would be routine surgery went horribly wrong, as Jenny developed an allergy to the treatment and died six days later.

Apart from the divorce of my parents in November 1986, the death of Jenny on 9 September 1980 had the most profound influence on my life and running career. It was to Jenny, not my mother or father, that I had turned for strength, guidance and love when I was small. It was Jenny who looked after me when my mother was desperately ill with a blood disorder; I was only four at the time. Growing up in a household often made unhappy by the widening gap between my parents, I always regarded Jenny as the strong one in the family. I slept in the same room as her and I would always go to her ahead of anybody else when I had a problem.

Of all the people around me it was Jenny who understood me best of all and my most vivid recollections of her come from my early childhood, like the time she taught me to swim by throwing me into the deep end. Then, the old maxim of 'sink or swim' applied and I had to struggle as best I could to keep afloat without swallowing too much water. Jenny was, of course, poised to leap in should I show the slightest signs of distress, but she was a hard taskmistress and as long as I kept my head above water, she stayed on the side of the pool as I learnt to swim the hard way.

It was the same after my foot operation. Jenny was never one to sit idly by, waiting for something to happen, and when the time came for me to get up and about, it was my eldest sister who prodded me into action. Strict, yet sympathetic, Jenny got me on to my feet again and back on the sports field, and the tie between us was just as strong after she married Barney Fourie in October 1979. The couple moved to a smallholding nearby and I spent

19

many happy hours helping Jenny in the garden, or sitting in the kitchen, the autumn sun glinting through the window as we drank huge cups of coffee and chatted.

Jenny had such a strong personality that Quintus, Cara and Estelle also turned to her for advice. She was so self-sufficient and clever, thoughtful and caring that everybody loved her. But she and I had a special bond between us, a relationship so strong that when she was taken from me so suddenly it was as though a part of me had died.

At thirteen and in standard seven I had not even thought about death. My life then was so uncomplicated and I wasn't particularly worried when Jenny, who had qualified as a nursing sister, went into hospital. None of us ever thought that she might be allergic to some part of the treatment she received for what the doctors thought might have been a malignant tumour. It could even have been the anaesthetic, but in six days she was gone and my life would never again be the same.

I only realized the severity of Jenny's condition when I wasn't allowed to visit her in hospital. I knew she was ill, but it still came as a terrible shock when Ma woke me at four in the morning to tell me Jenny had died.

How do you cope with death, particularly when it is so unexpected? Initially, I had great difficulty coming to terms with the fact that Jenny had gone; I felt numb and I could neither believe nor accept it. Her death made everything in my life, even eating and drinking, seem of secondary importance. Everything around me shrank and became small and insignificant and it felt as if my brain had been shattered. It was in order to put the pieces back together that I turned to my sport. Running was the easiest way to escape from the harsh reality of losing my sister because when I ran I didn't have to think about life or death. It helped blot out what had happened and by running away from my grief I was proving to Jenny that in athletics I had found something I could really do well.

Even now, not a day goes by without me thinking about

her. It's not something that goes away with the passing of the years – in fact it intensifies in a way – and when I am doing something I often wonder what she would say or how she would react. I was so devastated by her death that it took seven years before I gathered the strength to visit Jenny in the cemetery and put flowers on her grave. That was hard, visiting the cemetery for the first time, because it was so difficult to accept that somebody I loved so much was in that grave and it was only my Christian beliefs that saw me through.

I really missed Jenny when I was overseas, particularly at the time when my career was falling apart in 1988 and I was lonely and needed somebody with her strength to guide me. After my relationship with my father ended, I turned more to my sister Cara but, since my return to Bloemfontein in 1988, I have become much closer to Estelle. My mother has always been there for me, but in a different way. I get love from Ma and I love her; we are very close, but I don't go to her for the advice I got from Jenny.

I am lucky still to have Ma, Estelle, Quintus and Cara, but I can never forget Jenny. It was very difficult without her when my parents separated and I can remember thinking how she would have coped. There is no doubt that the loss of Jenny had a major effect on my running career. By escaping from her death I ran into world class and although my running was to bring me much heartache and unpleasantness, I'm sure Jenny was proud of me each time I did well.

3

The Red Bag

Numbed and deeply shocked by the death of Jenny, I found a degree of solace in my running. It didn't take the pain away – nothing could do that – but it helped fill the dreadful void in my heart. Running gave me a focal point as I wrestled with the magnitude of my loss and at the end of a hard training session I was more at peace with myself. The sense of hopelessness was slowly replaced by a desire to achieve: to prove that there was some meaning to life with all its harshness. I had found an escape route from my despair and I wasn't going to let go.

On 19 September, ten days after Jenny's death, I ran a 3,000 metres race in Bloemfontein and came fourth in 10:19.8, a long way behind Sarina Cronje, who clocked 9:32.9. 'Just wait,' I told myself. 'It won't be long before you will be running as fast as Sarina.'

I returned to my training with new vigour and won two races, over 1,500 metres and 800 metres in my home town before coming up against Stephanie Gerber over 3,000 metres in Bloemfontein. Stephanie cracked the ten-minute barrier with 9:59.9, while I was third with 10:06.5. At the same meeting I was second to Stephanie in the 800 metres in 2:17.3 and I knew afterwards that it would only be a matter of time before I became a member of the nine-minute class of 3,000 metres runners. But first I had to concentrate on the two shorter races and I got my 1,500 metres time down to 4:24.3 on 12 November, when I was again second to Stephanie.

Those performances gave me a lot of hope for 1981 and, still using my athletics as a cocoon to shield me from Jenny's death, I trained hard under Pieter's watchful eye. On 14 February I came third in the Free State senior 1,500 metres championship and six days later set my first provincial record. Again it was in Bloemfontein in the annual Bill Troskie meeting and my time of 4:20.7 was a Free State under-16 mark. Now I was starting to get somewhere and I won two more 1,500 metres races and an 800 metres event before the South African junior championships in front of my home crowd in April.

I was growing weary of snapping at Stephanie's heels and this meeting would prove to me that I had the ability to beat her and run into top class. It was my first major championship and the adrenalin was pumping as I lined up for the under-16 1,500 metres final on Friday 3 April. I was second to Stephanie again, although this time the gap was a lot closer, as I clocked 4:22.9 compared to my great rival's 4:22.0.

After the 1,500 metres final I didn't really bother about the 800 metres. Second place in the national championships was a good result for me and in my mind I had 'given' the 800 metres to a girl from Transvaal who had already won the 400 metres. She was, I thought, a lot faster than me and I would be content with whatever came my way. I particularly wanted one of the red sports bags that the winners received along with their medals, but I resigned myself to the fact that I would have to wait until the following year to win one.

I got through the 800 metres heats without any trouble in 2:15.33 and warmed up for the final intending to run hard but without anticipating anything exciting. I easily kept up with the leaders on the first lap and, with 300 metres to run, thought that the other girls were running too slowly. I put on a spurt and surged to the front of the field and, coming into the straight, I wondered why the others had not come back at me. I could see the line and it suddenly dawned on me that I was going to win. 'The red bag,' I thought as I raced triumphantly for the line. 'You are going to win a red bag.'

Winning the race was such an unexpected bonus that it took a while to sink in. Zola Budd was the South African under-16 800 metres champion: that was something special and, in later years, I was to rate that victory second on my list of career highlights, behind the 1985 world cross-country championship. I had run faster than my winning time of 2:11.9 – a 2:10.9 in Sasolburg eight days previously was my personal best – but it was the title that counted and my family were ecstatic. I was glad my parents were at hand to share what was for me an exquisite moment and my victory was reward for them both: Daddy for his support through the season and Ma for finding the time to ferry me to and from training every day while running the house and looking after the catering business.

Pieter, too, was elated, and he came to the house that evening to congratulate me. I had already shared the news with Stompie and, my tracksuit covered with hair, I accepted my coach's praise with a warm glow in every limb. I was the first member of Pieter's squad who had won him a gold medal in the South African championships and our relationship changed with that victory. Aware that I had the talent to do well, we took each other more seriously and began to develop a bond that would last for six years.

On the road, I won the Free State 10 kilometres championship in August and came a very satisfying second to Diane Massyn in the South African championships, while cross-country was to prove a happy hunting ground for me after my success on the track. I secured my second national title of the year with victory in the South African

24

under-16 championship in Cape Town and finished third behind Diane in the annual Prestige cross-country meeting at Pietersburg.

It was not, however, all roses and my old rival Stephanie Gerber brought me back to earth with a bump when track racing resumed towards the end of the year. We squared up over 1,500 metres in Bloemfontein on 14 November and, in my final race of the season, I was again forced into second place. Stephanie was first with a South African record of 4:18.8 to my 4:19.0; she didn't know it at the time, but that defeat was just the spur I needed.

Second again just wasn't good enough, and I was determined to do better. The solution was to train hard and in December and January I pushed myself to the limit. I was good, but I could be better and, with Pieter showing me the way, I increased my running up to 100 kilometres a week. That's a lot of training for a fifteen-year-old, but I had already developed the fierce competitive edge that was to bring me two world championships and a string of records, so that I willingly sacrificed everything in a ceaseless quest for excellence.

Running had taken on new meaning in my life. What had started out as a normal school activity and then become an escape following the death of my sister had now become a way of life. I had improved so rapidly that I gained a great deal of personal satisfaction from achieving the goals set for me and the beauty of it was that there was always another challenge. Records are set to be broken; there is always another race to win. My defeat at the hands of Stephanie Gerber gave me the final push I needed and two months of intense training would ensure that she never beat me again. In fact I would only lose one more race on South African soil, a 1,000 metres event in Bloemfontein on 7 February 1983, when I came second to Ilze Venter, beaten by 0.5 seconds as I clocked 2:37.9.

I didn't have to wait long for the pay-off and in Bloemfontein on 19 February 1982 I set a South African under-16 and under-19, 1,500 metres record of 4:09.1. That was followed by a national under-16 800 metres record of 2:06.5 in Sasolburg in March, a South African under-19 3,000 metres record of 9:05.70 in Pretoria in April, a 10 kilometres road running record of 33:36 in Bloemfontein in July and another under-19 South African 3,000 metres record of 9:03.5 in my home town in October.

On the track I won the national under-19 3,000 metres and 1,500 metres championships and, best of all, the senior titles over the same distances. I was still fifteen when I won the senior championships at the Coetzenburg Stadium in Stellenbosch and, after turning sixteen in May, won the South African senior 10 kilometres road championship in July and the national under-16 cross-country title in Alberton two months later.

The highlight of the year was learning that I was to be awarded Springbok colours for track and field. It was a proud moment when I put on the famous green and gold blazer, but the occasion was marred by a row between my family and my coach.

I was to fly to Johannesburg to compete in the Prestige track meeting as a member of the Springbok team and had intended returning to Bloemfontein by car with Pieter. But my school (Dan Pienaar had amalgamated with Sentraal High and was now known as Sentraal) wanted to roll out the red carpet for me at Bloemfontein airport after the athletics meeting and my parents decreed that I should fly home rather than travel by car. They won the argument and I came back by air to a wonderful welcome from the staff and pupils, but the disagreement took some of the shine off my pride at becoming a Springbok.

Another row, this time between my father and me, almost spoilt another magical moment for me in 1983, when I was in the middle of the best season I ever had in South Africa. It happened in Durban in April, when I was a member of the Free State team to compete in the South African junior championships and I spent the first

26

night with my parents instead of with the rest of the team in a hostel. The following day I was warned by Free State officials that I might be withdrawn from the championships unless I stayed with the team, but my father didn't like that idea one bit. He wanted me to stay with him and I ended up in tears as I tried to persuade him to change his mind. 'Don't be so upset,' I begged. 'Please let me run.'

Being stubborn, my father initially refused to budge, but he eventually relented and grudingly took me to the track, where he dropped me off with a huge suitcase stuffed with five days' clothing and left me standing there all alone. It was actually very comical arriving at the South African championships in such unlikely fashion and I always laugh when I look back at the absurdity of the situation. Pieter, thinking that my father would not yield and that, consequently, I would not turn up, was really pleased to see me and he helped me turn the incident to my advantage.

'It's simple,' he said. 'You either let what has happened affect you positively or negatively.' I chose the positive approach and used the incident to make me more determined than ever to succeed in a race which was to rank third on my list of career highlights. I had already set my first world junior record of 15:35.67 for 5,000 metres in Durban on 29 January and followed that with a world junior 3,000 metres best of 8:46.41 at Coetzenburg Stadium, but the 1983 South African 3,000 metres championship was the cherry on the top. Like many athletes, I keep a diary and have faithfully recorded every step I have run since 1980. My 1982 diary contains a page on which I stencilled '4:05' and '8:45', which were the next goals I had set myself for the 1,500 and 3,000 metres. The 4:05 would only come in 1984, but in Durban on 2 February 1983 I hit my 3,000 metres target of 8:45 with six seconds to spare.

My time of 8:39.00 broke my own world junior record by more than seven seconds; it gave me a South African senior record, the national under-19 championship and a terrific amount of personal satisfaction. The records were

27

nice and the title was nice, but it was reaching my goal that was really important.

I could not, however, share my joy with my parents, who had abruptly returned to Bloemfontein. It was a bitter blow knowing that they would not be at the track when I ran in the 1,500 metres two days later and I felt lost without them. My father, I thought, must still be angry over the fact that I had to stay with the Free State team and it was fellow-athlete Elizna van Zyl who consoled me on that lonely Saturday night. Feeling lost and sad, I shared the same bed with Elizna, but again I refused to let a family matter disrupt my running and two days later, on 4 April, I won the South African under-19 1,500 metres title and on 15 and 16 April, I successfully doubled in the national senior 1,500 and 3,000 metres championships.

The strength and stamina I had built up by racing these two events made it easy for me to keep chipping away at the world junior 5,000 metres record, which was, in retrospect, 'soft'. From 15:35.67 in January, I took it to 15:24.08 on 25 April in Stellenbosch and, when the season resumed, I recorded 15:10.65 in Port Elizabeth on 17 October. I ended a gratifying year on the track with a South African 1,500 metres record of 4:06.87 in Bloemfontein on 28 October and would only have to wait until the following February to reach the 4:05 mark.

On the road I set South African 16 kilometres records of 56:43 and 55:28 at altitude, and a 10 kilometres mark of 32:20, winning the 10 kilometres championship. I also maintained my grip in cross-country when, aged seventeen and competing in the senior section for the first time, I won the South African title and came first at the Prestige meeting, only to be snubbed by the Springbok selectors, who apparently thought I was too young to qualify for cross-country colours.

4
On Top of the World

I knew I was in good shape when I ran headlong into 1984. The previous year had been the most successful of my career, but although Pieter and I were looking for a fast time in the 5,000 metres at Stellenbosch on 5 January, I certainly wasn't expecting a 15:01. Mary Decker then owned the world record of 15:08.26 in what was a relatively new event for women and my previous best over the distance was more than two seconds slower at 15:10.65. My first race over 5,000 metres, on 29 January 1983 in Durban, had yielded a world junior record of 15:35.67, in Stellenbosch on 25 April I clocked 15:24.08 and I took a big chunk out of that with 15:10 at Port Elizabeth on 17 October. Running at altitude in Bloemfontein a week later clocked 15:38.75 and I proved that there was nothing wrong with my speed when I broke the South African 1,500 metres record with 4:06.87 in my home town on 28 October. For a girl of seventeen, those were pretty impressive credentials and everything pointed to a successful year in 1984. But although the signs were there, they didn't add up to a 15:01, particularly on a windy night in the Cape.

The crowd at Stellenbosch, however, seemed to sense something was in the air. They could probably tell from the determination in my face that I intended to run well, but I don't think anyone could have guessed beforehand that this was to be my big night, the biggest of my career so far. After all, it was only my fourth attempt at the distance and I had done only one track session before the race.

That was on 29 December when, after a lot of hard internal training, I did 5 x 1,000 metres with a two-minute rest period. My average in a good workout was 2:25.6 and that single session turned out to be all I needed on a night that was to change my life. I was so fit after training well in November and December – traditionally good months for me – that even the wind didn't bother me and my split at 1,000 metres was 2:54.3 after an opening lap of 69.2 seconds. The best thing about Stellenbosch is the seating arrangements for spectators. The front row is very close to what many South African athletes regard as their favourite track in the country and the crowd was wonderful that night. I could feel them urging me on as I went through 1,500 metres in 4:21.1 and the atmosphere was electrifying when the commentator announced that I was on world-record pace. An athlete often does not hear the stadium commentator during a race, but on that night it got through to me. 'Oh no!' I thought. 'How am I going to run another eight laps when I'm already so tired after four?'

That's where my conditioning came in. This was the pay-off for all the hours I had spent on the road in the previous two months, and my reward was the strength and speed I needed to reel off lap after lap. My split at 2,000 metres was 5:33.0 and after 3,000 metres it was 8:55.9. I was tired, desperately tired, yet still I held on and the 4,000 metres mark came up in 11:59.0. Just another 1,000 metres to go and I could rest . . . 800 metres . . . 600 metres . . . 400 metres. At the bell I was gasping for breath, thinking only of the finish and wishing the torture was at an end. But I couldn't allow myself to slacken off. 'Keep going, push yourself, you can do it': those were the thoughts that flashed through my mind on the final lap and I had difficulty comprehending my achievement when I saw the time. It was an incredible 15:01.83, beating Mary's record by 6.45 seconds. At seventeen I was the fastest woman in the world and as the news flashed around the globe I was to become one of the most sought-after women in the world.

What do you do with a hot property? You market it – and that's what happened to me. By breaking the world record (unofficially, because South Africa is not recognized by the International Amateur Athletic Federation), I became a superstar overnight and although I was unaware of it at the time, my father was the referee of the international race to get the Budd signature. Everybody wanted a slice of Zola's 'action' and while I continued to run and to run well, there was a flurry of activity behind the scenes.

As wave after wave of publicity threatened to drown me, I was fighting off a bout of extreme exhaustion. I couldn't train for a week after breaking the record and kept crying. There was none of the exultation I thought I would experience after breaking the world record and I was surprised as the offers poured in. American colleges wanted me; the Italians were keen and so too were the British. Prominent Johannesburg businessman Naude Klopper, the mentor of that great middle distance athlete Sydney Maree, contacted my father. Klopper had helped Maree, a black South African, secure American nationalization and Sydney became a client of Mark McCormack's giant International Management Group, probably the most successful sports management company in the world. Klopper told Daddy I needed an agent and he thought McCormack was the man for the job. My father, meanwhile, had teamed up with another businessman, Bill Muirhead, of domestic appliance company Defy. He arranged a sponsorship deal with Defy and Muirhead took over the role of adviser to the Budd family, while IMG's John Simpson explored how best to make use of my British ancestry. The *Mail*, too, was on the move. It sent special correspondent Brian Vine and athletics correspondent Neil

Wilson to South Africa with the sole intention of spiriting me off to Britain – if they could make the right deal with Daddy.

Wilson was later to reveal that it was John Bryant, then the *Mail*'s features editor, who first brought me to the attention of his editor, Sir David English. Writing in the July 1988 edition of *Athletics Today*, Wilson said Sir David agreed that I was a potential story and then wondered how much bigger it would be if the *Mail* could get me a British passport.

'It was,' wrote Wilson, 'Friday, 2 March 1984. Within hours Brian Vine, the *Mail*'s special correspondent, was putting the possibility of the *Mail*'s involvement to Zola's father, Frank Budd, over the telephone, and I was being deputed – without being put into the picture – to check with the IAAF and the British Board while in Gothenburg that weekend for the European Indoor Championships about the likely official response.

'It may be interesting, in the light of what has happened since, to relate that Women's AAA secretary, Marea Hartman, IAAF secretary, John Holt and Emanuel Rose, then chairman of the IAAF's technical committees, all confirmed that all Budd needed was a British passport. I can remember Miss Hartman's words clearly. "The day she walks into my office and shows me a British passport, she's a British athelete." '

My British roots were the key to my entry onto the world stage because I was the paternal granddaughter of an Englishman, Frank George Budd. He was a Londoner, while my maternal great-grandmother, Janet McGibbon, was the daughter of a Scottish couple.

Janet came to South Africa when her sister Margaret, married to Captain William Carding MC of the Royal Dragoons, was desperately ill. She nursed Margaret through the last months of her life and, when Margaret died, Janet married the captain and settled in Bloemfontein. My links with Britain were forged when the Cardings' daughter,

Joyce, married my grandfather. Frank George Budd had come to South Africa before the First World War to install printing machinery at *The Friend* newspaper. Marooned in the country by the outbreak of the Great War, he fell in love with Joyce Carding and they married in my home town of Bloemfontein in 1926. My grandfather became a photographer on *The Friend* before starting a process engraving business that my father was to inherit.

Perhaps I should have had an inkling of what was to come after the world record at Stellenbosch, but I was oblivious to Daddy's plans. I am different from many other sportsmen and sportswomen when it comes to achieving. I gain tremendous personal satisfaction from my running and in performing well, but when I do well I don't flaunt it. Breaking Mary's record was fantastic as I had idolized her, but I was not content to rest on my laurels. There was a full season ahead, other races to run, and I concentrated on the next event instead of basking in the glory of my success.

The next stop was Potchefstroom where, on 25 January, I won a 3,000 metres race in 9:07.42; then, five days later I won a mile in Bloemfontein in 4:37.52. On 6 February in Bloemfontein I reinforced my claims to world class with a world junior best and a South African record over 2,000 metres with a time of 5:44.4; and on 15 February, at my happy hunting ground in Stellenbosch, I did 9:03.8 for the 3,000 metres on a windy night. There was another world junior record at Bloemfontein on 20 February, this time over 1,500 metres when I clocked 4:05.81, and my race record after that reads: 25 February – 3,000 metres in Pretoria, 9:05.9; 29 February – 3,000 metres in Stellenbosch, 8:37.5 (world junior record and South African record); 5 March – 3,000 metres at altitude in Germiston, 8:52.84; 7 March – 5,000 metres in Port Elizabeth, 15:09.86; 16 March – 800 metres in Kroonstad, 2:00.9; 21 March – 1,500 metres in Port Elizabeth, 4:01.81 (world junior record and South African record); 21 March – 3,000 metres in Port Elizabeth, 8:54.7.

The discrepancies in my times at Stellenbosch and Port Elizabeth and those at Bloemfontein, Pretoria, Kroonstad and Germiston are the result of the effect altitude has on athletes. The thinner the air, the harder it is to run fast, so inland times in South Africa are invariably slower than those at the coast and it was particularly satisfying to break that world junior 1,500 metres record in Bloemfontein.

It was in Port Elizabeth the morning after I broke the world junior 1,500 metres mark and doubled in the 3,000 metres that I first knew something was afoot. I saw Daddy talking to two men I did not know and I thought it was strange. Who were they and what was so important? One of the strangers was a chubby Englishman who turned out to be Brian Vine, the other was Neil Wilson. They were the men from the *Mail* and all was soon revealed. 'How would you like to run overseas, Zola?' Daddy asked me after a lengthy conversation. 'There's a possibility we can get you to England and a British passport. You can even run in the Olympics.' I thought it was a silly idea and that nothing would come of it, but the *Mail* and Daddy persisted. Vine and Wilson came to Bloemfontein for about three weeks to continue negotiating with my father; looking back, I think it must have driven them crazy, because there's not much to do in my home town for journalists staying so long! At the end of their stay they told me that everything was fine, that I could get a British passport, get to Britain and run in the Olympics. It was as simple as that.

Simple? They made it sound so easy – get a passport, go to Britain and compete at Los Angeles. Daddy, the people from the *Mail* and Bill Muirhead were looking only at the short term and I don't think any of them considered me as a person or the implications of such a bold plan. How would a young, naive girl from the Free State cope in England? Had they considered the repercussions of a South African suddenly qualifying for Britain? What plans had been drawn up to counter the barrage of criticism that such action on my part would provoke in the British and South African media? How would I handle press conferences when I wasn't even bilingual?

Those were questions that would buzz around my head after my arrival in England and I wish they had been asked before my departure. At the time, though, I allowed myself to be drawn into the plan to run in the Olympic Games. My running then was really going well and although I was at the University of the Orange Free State, I was often training three times a day. That meant cutting classes, but I wasn't happy at university because my ambition was to go to a technikon to study personnel management. My unhappiness at university contributed, I think, to my agreement to go along with the 'Make Zola British' campaign. I was not enjoying university – I didn't like my subjects of political science, history, South-Sotho, ethnology and psychology and I didn't like the atmosphere – and I began to see going to Britain as a means of escape.

Contributing to my unease were the subtle undercurrents flowing between Pieter, the university coaches and me. While I wanted to go to the Bloemfontein technikon to study personnel management, Pieter persuaded me that I would be better off at university. Perhaps he was afraid of losing me yet, on the other hand, he indicated that the university coaches wanted me to break away from him and train under their direction. Pieter always protected his position as my coach and although I didn't like the whole set-up, I followed his advice and went to university. The catch was that Pieter had applied for a teaching post at the UOFS and, in retrospect, I think he felt he might have a better chance of remaining my coach if we were both at the same place.

If being able to quit university was one thing that made the idea of going to Britain more attractive, I can't deny that I got a thrill whenever I dreamt about the Olympics. Every young athlete imagines standing on the rostrum to the acclaim of a packed stadium, savouring a victory against the best runners in the world, and I was no different. My

35

training and racing were going so well that I could picture myself in a similar position and I even dared wonder what it would be like competing against Mary Decker, whose picture was then stuck up on my bedroom wall.

That said, I still had reservations about leaving everything I held dear to live in a foreign land. Because of my father's involvement with Bill Muirhead, I had come to think of him as 'Defy Daddy'. After all, Daddy benefitted from the Defy sponsorship he had arranged and had the use of the car I had got from the domestic appliance company as part of the deal. Daddy was adamant that I should make the break from South Africa – and so was Pieter.

My last race in South Africa was a 2 kilometres fun run in the Free State town Welkom; with all the arrangements made courtesy of the *Mail*, my parents collected me and we drove to Johannesburg on the final leg of the 'great escape'. Before that, though, I went for a short jog with Pieter the weekend before the Welkom race and I again expressed my doubts about the entire exercise. I'll never forget that day because we were in the middle of a severe drought. It was terribly dry and the air was almost yellow, but I didn't mind, because I loved the Free State. This was home and I plucked up the courage to tell Pieter I didn't think it was a good idea to go to England. 'Listen, Zola,' he said. 'We have gone this far, so you might as well go through with it.' So I did.

The arrangements went like clockwork and I went from Welkom to Johannesburg with my parents in a car piled high with luggage. We had told everybody that we were going on holiday and nobody knew what was afoot, not even my closest friends. If, however, they had seen the car they would have known immediately that something was going on because all those suitcases indicated that we would be gone for a long, long time. In Johannesburg we spent the night with my aunt and uncle, Ronnie and Joyce Evans, and the next day, Saturday 24 March, I stepped aboard Flight KL 594 on the way to a new life.

It was not to be a particularly happy life and, although the world 5,000 metres record that started it all should remain with me always as one of my greatest achievements, I will always view that race with a hint of regret. Back in 1984 the 5,000 metres for women was a relatively new race and Mary Decker's world record of 15:08.26 was not really that difficult. The 5,000 metres was, in fact, an easy race, the world record within striking distance of anybody who was in good shape. I have always told people since then that the 15:01 was about the worst thing that could have happened to me as it resulted in four years of trauma with a handful of bright spots in between: 5 January 1984 was probably the worst day of my life. I know that sounds terrible because people think it's wonderful to race well and it is nice. But that record focussed world attention on me and the phone never stopped ringing. It also brought the *Daily Mail* into my life and I did not enjoy being a puppet on a string.

5
Reluctant Briton

I was both excited and confused when we took off from Jan Smuts Airport in Johannesburg aboard the Dutch jumbo jet. The excitement was natural because I was going on a great adventure to another country where, I was assured by everybody except my mother, I would carve for myself a great athletic career. The confusion came from the fact that Pieter had stayed behind and would only join me later in England and I missed the comfort of having him around because he was the only person who at that stage seemed to understand my love of running. He was also the only person who could motivate me and we were a team. Without Pieter I felt lost. I bought myself one of those little hand-held computer games which took my mind off what was happening and I played it all the way to Schiphol Airport in Amsterdam.

Being of solid, Afrikaaner stock and, like me, very much at home in her beloved Bloemfontein, my mother was not keen on our journey into the unknown. But such was Daddy's dominance that Ma had no say in the matter and she had to go along with everything that had been planned, although she was against it from the start. She was not involved at all – I doubt she was even consulted by Daddy – and it's not surprising she was so negative about the trip. I said my goodbye to my brother and sisters, who were quite surprised by what we were going to do, but we didn't even cry because none of us quite knew what to expect.

At the airport we were shown into the VIP lounge to keep up the cloak of secrecy and we were always accompanied by Brian Vine and Neil Wilson. They were to become an integral part of my life in the early days in England and I felt I couldn't move without my *Mail* shadows.

My first flight on a jumbo jet was a big thrill and I also got a kick out of stopping at Nairobi. We weren't allowed off the plane, but I stood on the steps and looked around, fascinated to think that I was in another country. I had never been out of South Africa before and I longed to be able to see what lay beyond the airport buildings. The *Mail* men were, of course, everywhere, taking pictures of me every time I moved. I hated it and I started to dislike the portly monocled Vine. He was single-minded about himself and his newspaper. I suppose that makes him a good journalist, but he certainly didn't endear himself to me by the way he went about the 'Budd story'. Wilson was a little better – he certainly knew his athletics – but between them the pair had already incurred the wrath of my mother by using all the family photographs they could lay their hands on to use in their newspaper and in the 'official biography' which Vine was working on. The biography was another facet of the deal struck between my father and the *Mail*; on 'our' side, the pay-off was £100,000 and assistance in obtaining a British passport for me. Much was said at the time about the speed with which I got my passport, but what was overlooked was the fact that any minor with a claim to citizenship could obtain a travel document within fourteen days. More surprising for me was the arrival the day before we left for England of Daddy's passport. That application was processed really quickly.

I still had faith in Daddy then and I was aware that the contract involved a lot of money, because I was present when it was signed. Money then was, however, of secondary importance as I put body and soul into my athletics and I assumed that Daddy would do the right thing by me. It is ironic that not even my father fully understood how I functioned as an athlete and Vine didn't have a clue. As everybody knows, international athletics can bring the money rolling in and had I only been given the chance to get a passport without the payment by the *Mail* of a fat fee, I'm not sure Daddy would have been so interested in going to England. Money was very important to my father, while to Vine I was a source of material for his hungry typewriter.

For the *Mail*, I was the publicity scoop of the decade, as John Bryant would later recall on BBC Radio 4: 'You have to give credit to Sir David English for a story that would run and run. This must be one of the longest running and most headline grabbing news stories of all time. He spotted that story from a distance of 3,000 miles and saw its potential.'

The fact that I ran because I enjoyed it completely escaped notice. The newspaper executives assumed that the money and prestige they hoped I would acquire would motivate me once I was competing internationally when, in fact, it had nothing to do with my performances. Personal satisfaction, not a fat bank balance, counts most for a committed athlete and the only person who knew what I was going through was Ma. She was the one who took me to training in South Africa, she was the one who took me shopping, she was the only one who gave me love . . .

My first steps in Europe were taken in Amsterdam, where we switched to a ten-seater aircraft chartered by the *Mail*, which took us to Southampton. Poor Ma! She was really frightened when she had to get into the small plane, but she stood up to the trip gamely, just as she had weathered all the storms in the family prior to our departure.

After the clear, sunny skies of South Africa, my first impression of the land that was to become my home was the rain. It seemed to rain all the time which contradicted all the images I had built up from photographs I had seen.

You never see rainy pictures and I was struck by the grey skies and rows and rows of houses. It was also misty and cold, such a contrast to the warm country I had just left.

From Southampton we were driven to Brook, in the New Forest, where we holed up in a house, along with Brian Vine. I couldn't get away from the man and the constant tap-tapping of his typewriter was driving me mad. 'You have got to get rid of him,' I told my father. 'I can't train properly or do anything with this man in the house all the time.' It worked, because Vine moved elsewhere, but I was still homesick. The cold and damp did not agree with me and shortly after my arrival I phoned Pieter in Bloemfontein, where he was waiting to hear if my British citizenship application was going to be successful. I hated England at that time, I was upset by the *Mail*'s involvement in my life and I wanted to go home. 'I don't want to run here,' I told Pieter. 'It's horrible, I've had enough.' Pieter, to his credit, was sympathetic. 'Tell them how you feel,' he said. 'Tell them you don't want to run in the Olympics.'

Well, that didn't work. My father's reply was a flat 'no' and it was back to square one. That proved to me that Daddy had no inkling of what makes an athlete run, although Pieter could relate to my anxiety. Up until that stage Pieter had been in control of my career, but now it was Daddy's turn. After all, there was money, lots of it, to be made and he handled the purse strings and he made sure what the *Mail* wanted, the *Mail* got.

Losing control was the biggest mistake Pieter and I could make. Pieter knew how I functioned as an athlete and my life had revolved around Ma, my coach and my sport. Now, that control had passed into the hands of people who didn't know anything about me, or my attitude to athletics.

With everything going wrong I was off to a bad start within the first week in a new country. Ma was unhappy – she burst out crying on the day we moved into the house in the New Forest – and suddenly my life was full of strangers who burst in and took over. It got worse when the news broke in South Africa that I had 'defected'. Being branded a 'traitor' to the country of my birth hurt me more than anything else and I was getting desperate.

It got better when Pieter arrived and I was delighted to see him. We really got along well then, but even with him in England I still found it difficult to train in the cold and wet. Running in the snow was a novel experience, but all the time we had to operate under a cloak of secrecy lest reporters from a rival publication should track us down. It didn't take them long and in early April a journalist posing as an autograph hunter appeared outside the house. We told the *Mail*, but it was too late. Alerted to my presence in the New Forest, the media converged on the house and Pieter and I had no choice but to escape. We sneaked out of the back of the house, through fields and mud, and the *Mail* picked us up later. That was a bright spot during a hectic period. Another was getting a canary from the *Mail* when it became apparent, even to them, that I was longing for my animals in Bloemfontein.

The canary was named Brian of all things, and he was also part of the 'great escape'. When the *Mail* minders took us to a hotel close to Guildford they brought Brian along and I had to sneak him in inside my jacket and keep him in the bathroom so that people wouldn't notice him.

We stayed in the hotel for a few days and then decided to find somewhere more permanent. Neil took us for a drive and we eventually settled on a house in Guildford, but things were far from rosy on the home front. Ma was still upset and one evening she faked a faint, which sparked off a terrible row. The tension between my parents was awful and the whole household was under constant strain. Poor Ma hated every moment and, assuming that I would make it to the Olympic Games, she kept a piece of cardboard in the drawer next to her bed on which she scratched off all the days until the 3,000 metres final.

It wasn't surprising that the atmosphere in the house

affected me and it all became too much to handle. During one training session with Pieter in Stoke Park, when it was cold and rainy, I told him I wanted to go home, that I couldn't stay in England a moment longer. 'Come on!' he replied. 'You've come so far that you can't go back now. What would all the people in South Africa say?' Pieter was right and I felt that after all the reports I had heard about the negative reaction in South Africa to the news that I had come to England I wouldn't be able to face another barrage of criticism if I slunk back without having a fair shot at the Olympic gold medal.

But I was still feeling wretched. From the day I arrived in England I felt that my attitude towards athletics was being exploited. Running was precious to me, it was private, yet here I was committed to people who did not share my deep affection for the sport. As if that wasn't bad enough, my parents were in constant disagreement and they gave each other a really hard time – with me always in the middle.

The bitterness in the family reached crisis point and we eventually agreed on one thing: if my passport was not through by 23 April, we would all go back to South Africa. I hoped fervently the application would be delayed and I was heartbroken on 6 April when we heard I had been granted citizenship. That might sound callous now, and give more ammunition to the 'Zola used her passport as a flag of convenience' brigade, but at the time I was desperately unhappy. I would gladly have swapped places with anyone.

When my passport was ready, *Mail* editor Sir David English arranged a posh dinner at a tennis club, to which he invited British athletics officials such as Marea Hartman and Nigel Cooper. With great to-do Sir David handed the document to me – and I just looked at it. There was no elation at the clearing of another hurdle, just the realization that there was no going back. Had I been able to assert myself, I would have called the whole thing off, but Daddy and, to a lesser extent, Pieter, had sufficient influence

43

over me that I couldn't say, 'No, I've had enough.' I think Sir David was disappointed at my lack of enthusiasm, but I couldn't feel sorry for him. He had been part of the whole plan and I wasn't going to make it easy for him. I saw the passport as a document that symbolized how other people had used me for their own ends. Apart from the despair I felt that evening, my only vivid memory was, of all things, about the food. The pudding was delicious, meringue with walnuts.

I hope that one day Sir David will realize just what his newspaper put me through to get its exclusive story: the seemingly endless picture sessions, and the strain of trying to pretend I was British when, in reality, I was a young Afrikaans girl way out of her depth. The image the *Mail* portrayed of a girl with English ancestry coming back to her roots just wasn't true. It was all so pretentious and false. That wasn't me in the paper, it was somebody else.

It all seemed so unreal. 'Come on, Zola, you are British now and you must act the part.' Why, I wondered, couldn't the *Mail* tell the world that they had brought an Afrikaans girl with a legitimate claim to British citizenship to England? Tell them that I could not speak English properly and that I needed time to adapt? I'm sure that would have made it easier for people to accept me and it would certainly have made my life easier. I just wanted to be myself and I didn't want to be pushed. As it was, I was getting a hammering from both sides, with criticism in South Africa for deserting the land of my birth and howls of outrage from the anti-apartheid lobby in England because I had been given a passport.

Even now I find it difficult meeting and talking to people for the first time. It was worse then because nobody realized that I had been persuaded against my better judgment to come to England. I'm not saying that I would not have made the decision myself at some stage, but the timing was all wrong in 1984 and nobody was looking beyond the short term. With what seemed like most of the world calling for my head, it was natural for me to be skittish on

44

being introduced to someone new, because I was always unsure what their reaction would be. If they had an argument to pick, it wasn't so much with me as a person as with what they perceived me as representing. They didn't like the way I got my passport, they didn't like apartheid, they didn't like South Africa . . .

Forgotten amidst all the back-slapping by the *Mail* was the fact that I still had to function as a person and in addition to being homesick I was horrified at the lack of long-term planning that had gone into the 'Budd project'. Although I was the focus of all the attention, I felt as though I didn't count as a person and it got to the point where I lost my zest for running. That was unusual because I lived for my athletics, but from the day I arrived in England I hardly ever got in a full day's training. I missed a session here, another there and when things really started to get on top of me I ended up in tears. I didn't want to run, I didn't feel like running and Pieter tried valiantly to console me.

After every cry-session Pieter would talk to me and I would be OK for another few days until it started all over again. Poor Pieter, he tried everything to motivate me and nothing worked. I particularly hated training in the mornings, when it was cold, and one of his ideas was to set off ahead of me on a 10 kilometre run as if it was a handicap. His plan was for me to take the bait and try and beat him, but I took perverse pleasure in doing the opposite. I realized what he was up to and instead of running hard to beat him I just jogged along behind. I thought it was really funny at the time, although I must have driven Pieter crazy.

Nothing Pieter could say or do helped and I sank so far into the depths of despair that all I wanted was to go home. I wanted to go home yesterday but, stuck with the *Mail* contract and under pressure from my father I began to regard the Olympics as a symbol of my return to South Africa. I was fed up and I couldn't believe the attitude of the people around me. I don't know how Pieter thought he would continue coaching me after the Games and

45

no thought had been given to my movements after Los Angeles. Daddy had not bothered to discuss it with me and I was out on a limb. Would I stay in Britain or would I go back to South Africa? Who would be my trainer when Pieter went back to South Africa? Nobody had any answers and the Olympics became for me just another race. The balloon had burst during the turmoil of my first week in England and my dreams were shattered. All of a sudden I couldn't wait for the Olympics because then I would be able to go home.

6
Family Split

Racing was almost the last thing on my mind when I lined up at Dartford on 14 April 1984 for my first outing on a British track. I had been unable to concentrate on my running with all the outside pressure and I was fortunate to have had almost a full season in South Africa behind me. I also had the ability to race well, no matter how bad I felt, and I think Pieter knew that, even though I had not trained well since my arrival in England, I would not let him or the *Mail* down. The *Mail* had arranged for me to join the Hampshire club, Aldershot, Farnham and District and I was obliged to run because I had to meet the Olympic 3,000 metres qualifying time. It was a bit silly, really, because I had already done 8:37.5 in Stellenbosch two months previously, but that didn't count because South Africa was suspended by the International Amateur Athletic Federation. I had to qualify as a Briton, so Dartford it was.

When the people from the *Mail* first showed me a photograph of the track at Dartford I wasn't very impressed. It was a dirt track and it looked horrible, but what a transformation on race day! Realizing that the event would be televised, the race organizers had put a lot of work into getting the place neat and tidy, and it didn't look half as bad as my first impression from the photograph. But I still wasn't used to running on cinders and I had to wear spikes, horrible green ones, which was another minus. I didn't often bother with spikes, running most of my races in South Africa barefoot on synthetic surfaces and, to cap it all, they were sprinter's spikes I had received as a gift.

Coming from a farming background, I saw nothing out of the ordinary in running barefoot, although it seemed to startle the rest of the athletics world. I have always enjoyed going barefoot and when I was growing up I seldom wore shoes, even when I went into town. The exceptions were when I went to school or to church or on special occasions, and it was natural when I started running that I should do it barefoot.

I received my first pair of running spikes when I was thirteen and used them in a big inter-school athletics meeting. I found them uncomfortable and after that I decided to continue running barefoot because I found it more comfortable. I felt more in touch with what was happening – I could actually feel the track – and it wasn't until the cross-country season that year that I got my first pair of proper training shoes. Before that, I was content to run in plimsolls, or 'tackies' as the South Africans call them, if I was training on hard surfaces, but as most of the work I did was on grass I would usually be back to 'normal', barefoot. My first training shoes were Brooks, a company with which I was later to sign an endorsement deal, and it took several years to gain the confidence to tackle major races wearing spikes.

The newshounds were waiting for me outside the house on the morning of the Dartford race and, because it was still something of a novelty and I was overwhelmed by all the attention I was getting, I took pictures of the pressmen through the window. The *Mail* took me to a school ground a long way from Dartford to warm up so that it could maintain its exclusivity on my movements and it was there that I met John Bryant for the first time. Later to move to the *Independent*, John worked for the *Mail* in 1984 and he was to play a pivotal role in my career when, after the Olympics, I wanted to quit the international arena.

That was in November 1984 and John came to South Africa in an attempt to talk me into going back to Britain. Later, in 1987, John was again on hand when Fanie van Zijl decided I needed a British coach to take some of the pressure off me. It didn't look good politically for me to have a South African coach and John willingly posed as the 'front man' and actually took over as my coach after Fanie drifted out of my life when the chips were down and the IAAF were after my blood. I was to develop a good relationship with John: not as deep as the association I had with Pieter, but in a way more satisfying. John understood my needs more than either Pieter or Fanie and he came close to grasping what running really meant to me. It's a form of art when you run well and gaining enjoyment from what you are doing is everything. John seemed to appreciate that, which made a change from Daddy's attitude and that of Pieter, Jannie Momberg, Fanie and everybody else who was to climb on to the 'Buddwagon'.

I run because it is related to my well-being, both mental and physical. If I don't run I get depressed and if there were no races and no money I would still carry on with the sport I love so much. I see running as a way of expressing myself and I can't get the same satisfaction from anything else. Of course I have my 'off' days and sometimes I hate the training sessions. But the real pleasure comes afterwards: at the end of the day when I go to bed in the knowledge that I have achieved something for myself.

Although I was initially reluctant to compete internationally because it was virtually forced upon me, running has enabled me to travel and see something of the wonderful and stimulating world in which we live and that is one of the reasons why I kept coming back to South Africa to train. Bloemfontein may not always provide ideal training conditions – in summer, temperatures can reach between 36-40°C and in winter the mercury can plummet to –5°C –

49

but I enjoy the extremes of hot, cold, wet and dry and train best and feel most comfortable in those surroundings.

That was part of my problem in England – the weather was so bad. There's not much enjoyment to be gained from training in what somebody born and raised in a country like South Africa regards as a 'hostile' environment. A fine summer's day in England takes a lot of beating, but they were so few and far between that I was constantly drawn back to a part of the world that I felt comfortable in. In South Africa you can smell the soil when it rains and you can even smell the rain. In England, though, everything smells the same. Give me warm weather and I train and run well; but put me where it's grey and damp and I find it difficult to keep my athletic standards high. That was one of the reasons I kept coming back to South Africa to train, even though I knew it was an act that was to give my opponents all the ammunition they needed to shoot me down. Other British athletes can train wherever they like, but not Zola.

In view of the emotional upheaval I had been subjected to after my arrival in England and the fact that I was still acclimatizing to a country in which I had little affinity with nature, my performance in my British début wasn't bad at all. The *Mail* had done a good job in finding for me a secluded spot where I could warm up and I did all my stretching and jogging. When the time came to go to Dartford, Pieter called me aside and gave me some advice I have never forgotten: 'All the calmness is over now and you have got to prepare yourself for the future.' At first I didn't understand what he was getting at, but I soon found out when I got to the track.

As an athlete I was accustomed to big crowds and an electrifying atmosphere, but I wasn't prepared for Central Park in Dartford. It was scary being singled out as the focus of attention and I needed a police escort to get to the track. I was so self-conscious that when Pieter, who was sitting with the spectators on the outside of the track, called me and said I should do some strides, I refused. 'No,' I said,

'I'm too embarrassed in front of all these people.' Without a final warm-up, I went straight into the race and I didn't enjoy my British début one bit because it was so boring. I couldn't concentrate and the race seemed to take ages, although I won comfortably enough in 9:02.6. Compared to my performances in South Africa, that was slow, but it was still a British junior record and an Olympic qualifying time.

I was given flowers after the race and then it was time to face the media in my first real press conference. This exposed a flaw in the *Mail*'s planning, because I hadn't been 'coached' in the art of fielding reporters' questions and I found the whole thing confusing and frightening. Sitting in front of a battery of cameras, I was asked about things I had never even thought about – politics, apartheid, my attitude to running – and I left Dartford bemused by the whole experience. I hadn't been in the right mood for the race and I wasn't particularly pleased with my performance, but everybody else was happy and I was able to relax on the way home when we stopped at a tea-shop.

Tea-shops were to become my favourite haunts in England. I can drink tea until the cows come home and I love the atmosphere in tea-shops. On this occasion half my gear was in one car and the rest in another and I didn't have any shoes. No problem for me: I went in barefoot as I would have done in Bloemfontein, but I got some strange looks. 'Oh dear,' the people inside seemed to be saying, 'the poor child. What's she doing in here without shoes?'

Now that I was firmly established in the headlines as Britain's new running sensation, it didn't take long for race offers to come pouring in. Pieter and I had a visit from British athletics promoter Andy Norman and Oslo promoter Swen Arne. They were both very nice and friendly and suggested a racing schedule for me that included a 10 kilometres road race in Oslo. It was a new experience meeting people such as Andy Norman, who talked about Seb Coe and Steve Ovett in matter-of-fact terms without alluding to their greatness. Still young and impressionable, I tended to put athletes of that calibre on a pedestal because to me they seemed almost superhuman and I had not stopped to consider that they also led ordinary lives just like the rest of us.

The shoe companies were also after me and, being new to the 'game', I hadn't even considered product endorsement. So it came as a surprise when the companies came to visit and I started building up quite a selection of running shoes, spikes and clothing. I must have driven them crazy then, because in my early days in England I would mix and match, wearing Adidas shoes with Nike tops, or Brooks shoes with Adidas tops. The Nike representative was first to call, but I'll never forget the day Mel Batty of Brooks arrived because the whole house was full of shoes. I liked Mel at first sight and was to have a lot to do with him as my career in England blossomed and I became a member of the Brooks 'stable' of sponsored athletes.

I was, however, first and foremost *Mail* property until my contract expired in November 1984 and I was lucky to have Neil Wilson on my side. After I was selected for the British team I had another of those dreadful picture sessions when, dressed in my British kit, I had to pose for the *Mail* cameraman on Merrow Common in full view of everybody going by. One photograph after another; it seemed it would never end, but there was nothing I could do about it except keep smiling. In an attempt to get as much mileage from me as possible, the *Mail* even tried to get me to make a brief sortie into the fashion world. They wanted me to model some of the latest clothes, but John Bryant, thankfully, put a stop to that. It had been bad enough running through daffodils in the New Forest and parading my British colours, but I drew the line at switching from athlete to fashion model. At that stage I didn't even wear make-up – I still use very little – and my favourite form of dress was, and still is, tee-shirt and trousers.

In the midst of my settling-down period it was lovely to see my sisters Estelle and Cara and brother Quintus, who came to England to visit. They came bearing gifts in the form of biltong, jam, mealie pap and dry boerewors, all wrapped up as presents to elude the customs officers. What a feast we had! Biltong is meat that has been dried and spiced like the American version of jerky; mealie pap is maize meal, made into a stiff porridge; and boerewors is a special kind of South African sausage. They are all traditional Afrikaans foodstuffs and we had a grand time unwrapping everything and gorging ourselves. Quintus had his camera with him and took loads of photographs and we compared notes as I had become a keen photographer. I had taken up photography because I had stopped studying to concentrate on my athletics and I needed an outlet. I bought an Olympus camera and snapped everybody and everything.

I also had Johnny, a cat I was given by John Simpson, of IMG's London office. Johnny eventually came back to South Africa with me after the Olympic Games, but 'he' had a dark secret. 'He' came to me as a male about a month after I arrived in England and was christened as such, but then subsequently had kittens. It was too late to change 'his' name, so Johnny she remained and I love her dearly. She gave everybody a hard time, climbing the neighbours' trees and generally getting in the way. Once, Johnny got lost and we put up a notice that had all the children in Merrow Park prowling around looking for her. They found her and she came back black from her nose to the tip of her tail after finding her way to the railway tracks.

On the running front, I won a 1,500 metres event in London on 25 April and then it was off to Oslo for a 10 kilometres road race. This was an important race for me because it was my first real test against truly international competition – Grete Waitz and Ingrid Kristiansen were in the field – and I knew from time trials that I was in quite good shape. Our party comprised Pieter and Carin, John

Bryant and myself; we had to go without my parents because, being South Africans, they had problems with visas. Pieter and his wife, Carin, managed to get into Norway on some kind of emergency visas, which caused a lot of trouble for Swen Arne afterwards. The Norwegians were not happy about having South Africans in the country and it was probably because Pieter and Carin got through the border that I was never invited back to Oslo. At the time, though, nothing could dampen my excitement. This was my first trip outside England and I was fascinated by everything I saw.

But my exhilaration was to be short-lived. The Press were everywhere; I couldn't move without them, and they put me through the mill at a press conference in Oslo. At that time I still had dual South African and British citizenship. I hadn't had time to relinquish my South African citizenship and the fact that I was a dual citizen resulted in lots of sticky questions.

As a *Mail* man, John Bryant sat beside me at the conference to field the questions and that was a big mistake. One of the journalists immediately wanted to know what right he had to decide what they could and could not ask. It was as much a vendetta against the *Mail* as it was against my taking up British citizenship, and after they had finished with John they turned to politics. I felt like South African Minister of Foreign Affairs Pik Botha and was asked such questions as: 'Well, Zola, how do you feel about running against black people?' That really showed up their ignorance and I replied that in South Africa the majority of athletes were black, especially in road running. Athletics in South Africa had been integrated for years, but the journalists had not bothered to check their facts. South African athletes are just that – athletes – and the colour of an athlete's skin has absolutely no bearing on the sport. I certainly never worried who I lined up against; they could have been green for all I cared, because it was only the competition that mattered.

Trailed constantly by reporters and photographers, I became so weary of the media that when the British contingent in Oslo went to look at the course I initially refused to go. Andy Norman talked me into joining the other British athletes and they were wonderful. They must have realized what I was going through and were very kind and helpful. I had no idea then that the media could be so hostile and bothersome – ironically the journalists who gave me a really hard time represented South African publications – although I can forgive the photographer who took a lovely picture of me with Grete Waitz. He gave me a copy and I have treasured it ever since.

The race went well for me after a slow first 5 kilometres and I followed Ingrid when she surged at 7 kilometres, managing to hang on although I was beginning to feel very tired. Going up a hill I started coughing a bit; Ingrid ran away from me and Grete fought back to take second place. But I was pleased with my time of 31:42 on a tough, hilly course. It was a personal best time and highlighted the paradox of being able to enjoy a good race while, at the same time, being unhappy about the situation in which I found myself. On the one hand I wanted to return to South Africa, on the other I relished the chance of rubbing shoulders with stars like Grete and Ingrid. Talk about having your cake and eating it!

The cake I didn't want to eat was the one the *Mail* gave me for my 18th birthday on 26 May. A fruit cake, it had green icing with a track on top and a figure that was supposed to be me. The cake was another *Mail* publicity ploy and I was duly photographed celebrating with a cake which, for me, was the ultimate in bad taste. Not so the mouth-watering delicacies Estelle, who was back in England to see the family, conjured up in the kitchen in Guildford. They were lovely and I stuffed myself until I could hardly move.

Also in England for about a month were Springbok steeplechaser D.B. Prinsloo and top South African middle

55

distance runner Elizna van Zyl. They came over so that I could have some company and good training partners and I thought the time had come when I could finally get in a week of solid training without any interruptions. How wrong I was as the tensions in the Budd family finally exploded.

My parents were not getting on well at all and things were very tense in the house. While Ma was especially unhappy, Daddy was having a wonderful time seeing his relatives and enjoying the attention he was getting as the father of Britain's latest running sensation. Daddy was still involved with Bill Muirhead, of Defy, and part of my sponsorship package in South Africa included a car from Defy, ostensibly for my parents to use for getting me to and from training and athletics meetings. We also got clothing bearing the Defy label and I think there was money involved. Such was Daddy's preoccupation with Muirhead that I started thinking of him as 'Defy Daddy' and I was upset when my father took the car for his own use. Ma was stuck with the old family car to take me to training while Daddy drove everywhere in 'his' nice new one.

It was in Guildford that I tumbled to the fact that Daddy and Muirhead were still working closely together. Unable to run properly in the strained atmosphere at home, I went to an estate agent to investigate the possibility of buying a flat – with only one bedroom so that I could escape from Daddy's clutches. I saw just what I wanted in Merrow Park, but when I approached Daddy about buying it he refused point-blank to consider the matter.

Earlier, he had wanted me to buy a house in Birmingham, but I wasn't keen on the idea. After all, we had just settled in Guildford and I didn't want to move to another part of the country, but I did want to get out of the house. Perhaps his refusal to let me live on my own was his way of getting back at me for not going to Birmingham and there was nothing I could do about it. Although the money he

56

My first birthday.

One step ahead of old rival Stephanie Gerber on my way to victory in the under-16 1,500 metres at the annual Bill Troskie in Bloemfontein in February 1981. A Free State junior record of 4:20.7 was the reward for a lot of hard training as I used athletics to fill the void in my life left by the death of my sister Jenny five months previously.

I win the first 'big' race of my career, the under-14 1,200 metres at the Free State inter-school athletics championships in 1981. This was one of the proudest moments of my career.

In pole position on the inside lane during the South African senior 1,500 metres championship in my home town of Bloemfontein in April 1983. Still sixteen, I won the race in 4:10.13 from Eranee van Zyl (No. 72).

Signing autographs after breaking the world junior 5,000 metres record with a time of 15:10.65 in Port Elizabeth in October 1983.

With British officials Nigel Cooper and Marea Hartman on the day I received my British passport.

Getting used to my new surroundings in England.

A pep talk from coach Pieter Labuschagne.

(Opposite) Digging deep into my reserves of speed and strength, I concentrate on maintaining the pace on that windy night in Stellenbosch in January 1984, when I broke Mary Decker's world 5,000 metres record.

Staking my claim for a place in the Olympic team, I came out of hiding to win the 3,000 metres at Dartford on 14 April 1984 in a British junior record of 9:02.6.

One of the perks of being a top class runner is landing sponsorship deals which make life a lot easier. I had the use of this car when I was running well in England, but had to return it when I lost form in 1986.

With coach Pieter Labuschagne at a Press conference in Oslo before the 10 kilometres road race against Ingrid Kristiansen and Grete Waitz in May 1984. I had a tough time answering questions from aggressive journalists, but it was a thrill competing against two of the world's greatest athletes and I finished third in a personal best time of 31:42.

*In the bunch in the early stages of the 3,000 metres final at the Olympics
in Los Angeles in 1984 with (from R-L) Mary Decker, Maricica Puica and
Wendy Sly, the main protagonists in the drama.*

The fall. I struggle to maintain my balance as Mary Decker goes sprawling. Wendy Sly is on the extreme left and Maricica Puica, the eventual winner, is directly behind me.

Looking at the anguish on Mary's face as she is helped off the track after her fall, I can understand her feelings of frustration and anger.

A distraught Mary Decker on the infield at the Memorial Coliseum after tumbling out of contention.

was holding from Defy and the *Mail* was rightfully mine, Daddy would not let go of the purse strings and I was stuck. I was appalled when I overheard a telephone conversation during which he discussed the situation with Muirhead. I felt he had no right to discuss my affairs with Muirhead without consulting me, yet here he was mapping out my future.

Each incident built up to a climax and my relationship with my father reached breaking-point when I was invited to a braai with people from the South African Embassy. A power struggle developed between Daddy and Pieter, with Daddy wanting me to accept the invitation and Pieter advising me to turn it down. I don't know what motivated either of them to take the stand he did, but I was in the middle, being pulled this way and that. I was drawn into the quarrel and when I could take no more of the arguing I 'disappeared'.

I had to get away from the eternal wrangling, so I jumped on my bike and rode to the golf course, where I sat for an hour and savoured the luxury of being alone. I wanted them all to worry about me and when I left the golf course I went to see a movie in Guildford. It was terrible sitting in the cinema all by myself all afternoon, but I wanted Daddy to learn his lesson and I only headed for home in the early evening. He had, and everybody was out looking for me. Daddy met me on the road and apologized for the way he had acted. But, at the same time, the battle lines had been drawn. My father told me he would never do anything to hurt me and that he just wanted what was in my best interests. He made Pieter out to be the culprit; yet with Pieter it was the other way round. As far as Pieter was concerned Daddy was to blame. I was gradually manoeuvred into the position of having to make a choice. Daddy or Pieter, who would it be? I needed them both for different reasons, but I couldn't carry on like this.

It was another invitation, this time from Pieter and Carin, that decided the matter. Two weeks before the

57

Olympic Games Carin and Elizna went to see my father to ask if I could attend a fondue at the Labuschagnes' house. Daddy was furious, I think he resented the fact that Pieter was exerting so much influence over me, and he had a nasty row with Carin. What right, he demanded, did Carin and Pieter have to organize my life? Nobody likes being yelled at so Carin gave as good as she got before Daddy slammed the door in her face. I was devastated when I heard about the row; for me it was the last straw as Daddy had also been nasty to Ma, although I must admit that my mother can be difficult at times, and he and I had been arguing. There was no way I could continue my Olympic build-up with so much antagonism in the air, and the fondue incident forced the choice upon me.

The slamming of the door symbolized the end of my relationship with my father and I walked out of the house. Just like that. I had had enough and I packed my things and telephoned Pieter to ask him if he would take me in. My coach came and collected me and I wrote to Daddy, telling him that I didn't want him in Los Angeles for the Olympic Games. This time he had gone too far and we didn't speak again until after the Games. I still continued to visit Ma, first ringing her up to make sure Daddy was not around, but the rift between my father and me was too deep and wide to bridge. My English aunt and uncle, Ronnie and Joyce Evans, tried to reconcile us, but I wasn't interested, not after my mother told me that my aunt had said I was a 'real bitch'.

Elizna and D.B. were caught in the middle of the Budd domestic squabble and my friendship with Elizna became strained. But it was a lot of fun at first having them around, and I shared a room with Elizna. She was good for me and helped calm me down when I got upset, as on the day I packed everything up and told her that I was finished with England and determined to return to South Africa. Elizna just sat on the bed and laughed at my hysterics, which effectively brought me back to earth.

It had been tricky seeing Elizna for the first time after her arrival in Britain because when we had parted in South Africa, I had told her I was going on holiday. 'Bye,' I had said, 'see you soon.' Elizna knew nothing about our plan and must have been annoyed when she heard about it as Pieter had also been her coach and she had been in the middle of a good season. Pieter dropped her to come with me to England and it was an act of real friendship for her to come over to see me and help me with my training. D.B. was a super training partner who, unlike many male athletes, never tried to demonstrate his superiority when we were running together. Sometimes the three of us trained three times a day and, when we were not running, we went sight-seeing and had braais. Sadly, the fight with my father changed that. Elizna was still living with my parents and after that incident my relationship with her cooled a little. We had a lot of good times together, though, and I think both Elizna and D.B. thoroughly enjoyed their stay in England.

Back on the track, things were going quite well. I won the British 1,500 metres championship in 4:04.39 at Cwmbran in Wales, setting a European junior record, and I was first home in the 3,000 metres at the Olympic Trials at Crystal Palace on 6 June, setting another European junior mark of 8:40.22. The trial was, for me, just that, as I ran the gauntlet of all the anti-apartheid demonstrators who had been assembled for the occasion. We used the back entrance to get into the stadium so that I could warm up and there were police everywhere to contain the 'rent-a-crowd'. But they couldn't prevent the demonstrators from shouting, and I faced the starter with 'racist scum' and 'fascist bitch' ringing in my ears and ran the race to a cacophony of booing and cheering. It wasn't surprising, therefore, that in my diary I recorded the fact that I 'could not concentrate' and that 'actually, I could have gone faster'.

After the Olympic Trial, I won races in Belfast (3,000

59

metres in 8:51.99) and Birmingham (1,500 metres in 4:14.22) before what was to be a landmark race for me at Crystal Palace. It was the 2,000 metres in the Peugeot–Talbot Games in London on 13 July and my last competitive outing before the Games; everything was set for a world record attempt. A pacer had been arranged and the only problem was Zola: I didn't want to run. On the way to the track in the car with Pieter, I used what was then my stock argument when I was feeling down: 'I'm not feeling well and I don't want to do this race', I told him. Bang, yet another explosive situation between reluctant athlete and determined coach! Our fights usually started this way, with me telling Pieter I was not interested in running internationally . . . I just wanted to go back to South Africa. His reply was that this was my big chance and I should make the most of it. If I didn't, I would end up on a smallholding in Bloemfontein with my mother; if I didn't run, I as a person would not count; if I didn't run well, I would amount to nothing.

Until my injury in 1986, I always ended up believing Pieter and accepting his point of view, but it was emotional blackmail and on the way to Crystal Palace we ended up screaming at each other. Pieter told me afterwards he was so furious that he felt like driving the car into a tree. He was after a world record and here I was being so negative. I can't blame him for getting so angry, because he was in a difficult position with a temperamental athlete on his hands, but he should at least have shown some consideration for my feelings. I ended up in tears and had I been the coach, I would never have let an athlete who was so obviously desperately unhappy compete.

We were to meet Neil Wilson on the way to the track and I sat in the car hoping mournfully that Neil would be late and I wouldn't have to run. We weren't late and I did have to run, but I was strangely detached as I warmed up. Pieter was, however, banking on the fact that I had always been able to pull something out of the hat and I didn't let him down. In spite of the tears beforehand, I won the race

60

with a sprint in a time of 5:33.15, which was a world record, and an added bonus was a world junior record of 4:30.7 at the mile mark.

A good run could not, however, entirely make up for the ordeal of forcing myself to perform well against a backdrop of emotional upheaval. It had required enormous mental strength to get out there and be aggressive and I had got into a terrible rut from which it was difficult to extricate myself. A world record was great, but not the hassles that went with it. Instead of looking forward to it, I had gone into the race regarding it as a means to an end: 'Get this over and then you just have the Olympic semi finals and final before you can go back to South Africa', I told myself. That was the wrong attitude and I was lucky it didn't last too long. My moods changed quickly and there were times when I really got excited about running in Los Angeles, like the occasion when I collected all my kit in London. Then, I was proud to slip on the British blazer and I got a kick unpacking everything at home and showing it off to Ma.

Given time to work things out myself, there is no doubt that I would have settled down and adapted to my nationality change. But I needed to go at my own pace without being under the pressure of the *Mail*'s 'Be British' attitude. Pieter's disposition didn't help either: he was beginning to lose track of what running meant to me and what motivated me, and a combination of these factors and the fight with my father took the shine off my great Olympic adventure. My desire to run was gradually being soured, like a jug of milk having lemon juice squeezed into it drop by drop.

7

Countdown to Disaster

It was with a feeling of relief that I saw Pieter off at the airport a few days before I was due to leave for Los Angeles with the British team. It wasn't as though I wanted to get rid of him – he was still my coach and mentor and I relied on him for everything connected with my career – but his departure signalled for me what I considered to be the start of the final act. 'The Olympic countdown has started', I thought as we drove to the airport with Pieter's brother, Jan. 'Soon this will all be behind me.'

It's odd that I always associate events with the weather and I remember that particular day being misty, but warm. I liked warm weather and with Daddy out of my hair the forecast for the Olympics seemed a little brighter. I was staying in Pieter's house in Merrow Park with Jan and his wife Trudi – Carin had returned to South Africa for a short visit before flying to Los Angeles. Jan and Trudi were very good to me and the pressure on me lifted almost as quickly as the mist disappeared under a hot sun. I spent a lot of time with Ma and even started enjoying my training. Without Pieter around there was nobody to tell me what to do, how to do it, when to do it or how hard to do it and I relished my new-found 'freedom'.

Not even a shower of rain while I was out on a 5 kilometres run in the woods could dampen my spirits as I began concentrating on the job in hand. I was moving easily and effortlessly, almost flowing through the woods, and I regained a lot of confidence. Listening to the birds calling and the leaves rustling, jumping over logs and feeling the mud sucking underneath my feet, I started thinking about the Games in a new light. Images rolled through my mind as I wondered what America would be like, what I would do in the Olympic Village, what clothes I should pack.

That was my last run in Guildford before following Pieter across the Atlantic Ocean. John Bryant drove me to a hotel near Heathrow airport. As usual, I had forgotten something, this time my toothbrush, and I had to hunt for a shop in the hotel to buy another. I met former Olympic Games long jump champion Lynn Davies, now an official, at the hotel and he was very good to me. We trained together in the afternoon and when Lynn told me after a session of fartlek that I was running quite well, I felt really good. It was just the confidence booster I needed and Lynn's kindness helped quell the butterflies in my stomach. We went for another run the following morning and then it was time to leave.

The butterflies started again as we approached Terminal Three at Heathrow airport and I couldn't believe the chaotic scene that greeted us. It was pandemonium, with British team members, luggage and the media all over the place. There were TV cameramen and photographers everywhere and I trusted to luck that my baggage would be loaded on to the right plane as British official Nigel Cooper helped me check in.

What a relief it was to escape from the throng and board the aircraft! I settled down and either watched the movie or read a book, unaware that an equally raucous reception awaited us in Los Angeles. I had taken some oranges with me and when we landed somebody told me that you are not allowed to take fruit into the country. I spent an agonizing sixty minutes waiting to clear customs, keeping my fingers crossed that they wouldn't search my bag and confiscate my oranges, and then ran the gauntlet of the press. There seemed to be hordes of pressmen everywhere and in an effort to escape one of the members of the British team dashed through the throng with a trolley, sending cameras flying.

From the airport we went by bus to the holding camp at Point Loma in San Diego and my first impression of America was the wide streets and huge motor cars. I was jet-lagged and terribly tired, but I perked up when I saw Pieter. Even though he was a South African, Pieter managed to get access to the holding camp because he was my coach, although first he was put to the test by black British javelin-thrower Tessa Sanderson. We were later to become good friends, but Tessa couldn't resist probing Pieter for any sign of racial prejudice. Pieter was sitting on a couch at Point Loma with a tiny place next to him; Tessa came along and plonked herself down. She began chatting and laughing and must have been pleasantly surprised when Pieter responded in similar vein. Tessa went out of her way to be nice to me and we exchanged gifts – I bought her a fluffy toy to wish her good luck and she gave me a toy husky dog.

Pleased as I was to see Pieter, we soon started clashing again when he saw other people with whom I came into contact as a threat to his status as my coach and friend. It was almost as if he was jealous if I did things with other people without his knowledge and one incident concerned Lynn Davies. We got along very well together and Lynn told me all about winning the Olympic gold medal in 1964, which helped boost my confidence for the 3,000 metres. One morning I was, as usual, up and about early and I bumped into Lynn. We went for a walk and had a lovely chat, but when I got back Pieter was in one of his moods. His attitude was that if he was my coach, why didn't I go for a walk with him? If I wanted to spend time with somebody, then surely I should do it with him? I couldn't work out what had got into him – perhaps he was just being

64

protective – but, because I respected him, I decided I had better do what he wanted. But that put me in a difficult position regarding Lynn and I started avoiding him and a lot of other people, which made me feel bad. I felt especially guilty about Lynn, who I like to think had become my friend, and I retreated back into my shell as I tried to work out just who I could speak to without upsetting my coach.

Pieter, Pieter, Pieter. I was being stifled by the closeness of our relationship, and I started to get my own back. Some of the security guards at the holding camp were really quite attractive and I couldn't stop talking about them. It annoyed Pieter, even made him jealous, but it was hard to resist the temptation to give him a hard time. I used to talk to the guards in the entrance hall whenever I went down to the vending machines and was happy to pose for pictures with two of them I had got to know quite well.

After I had been at the camp a week, Carin arrived; I was delighted to see her because she took Pieter off my hands. I needed some time away from him because I was finding him domineering, but I wasn't trying to get rid of my coach. I relied on Pieter because he knew what made me tick and we were a team. I appreciated the sacrifices he had made in an attempt to give me my big chance – it was a big step for him to give up his teaching post in South Africa and bring his wife overseas – and I respected him. That said, though, I still needed more freedom, time by myself when I could make new friends, and I didn't get it until Carin arrived in America.

I was more relaxed after Carin's appearance and the three of us had fun together. One of the things I love is food – lots of it – and I made the most of some of the excellent restaurants in San Diego. Although I am small in stature, there is nothing wrong with my appetite and I can eat almost anything without putting on weight. Just a week before the Games started I joined Pieter and Carin and John Bryant at a restaurant on the waterfront and I had

65

a huge meal of steak, salad and apple pie. No one who saw me on that occasion would have guessed I was training for the 3,000 metres final. I ate so much I could hardly move, but it didn't affect my running.

My training on the final run-in to the Olympics was going well at that stage. At one area we used there were eucalyptus trees which have a special smell all of their own and, although indigenous to Australia, are grown extensively in South Africa. Finding eucalyptus trees in San Diego was a bonus, like seeing a friendly face in a crowd of strangers, and their fragrant scent reminded me of Bloemfontein each time I ran through them. Little things like that are important when you are away from home, and I take comfort from them when I am feeing low.

The warm weather contributed to my well-being, as I sharpened up under Pieter's eagle eye. I did the majority of training on my own and we were always hunting for sports grounds or parks where I could run on grass, preferably barefoot. Sunshine was a tonic for me after the grey skies of England, and I became much more positive about the Games. The spring was back in my step, and I had no trouble getting up early to do about forty minutes of road work most mornings; I knew I was approaching the physical condition necessary for me to run well in the 3,000 metres after a really good track session. The day after running 300-metre repetitions, Pieter asked me to do two 1,000-metre runs in what should have been my final track workout, about a week before my big moment in the semi-finals, and I performed better than either of us could have hoped. I ran the first one in 2:40 and told my coach I was too tired to do another. He was having none of that. 'Come on,' he said, 'you can't possibly be too tired. You must do another one.' Once I had caught my breath, Pieter sent me off again. This time I ran inside 2:40, which was good for me, and I felt a glimmer of hope as I visualized the race.

Disaster was, however, just around the corner. With

my track work supposedly over, I was just keeping loose with strides, but a couple of days later Pieter saw that other athletes were still on the track. Although I had hardly ever done more than two track sessions he thought it would be a good idea for me to put in another. It wasn't on our schedule, but I did it anyway, and during the session I felt a twinge in my right hamstring. Initially I thought nothing of it, but then I found difficulty doing my stretching exercises. 'I'm sore,' I told Pieter. 'There is something wrong with my leg. I can't do all my exercises.'

My coach was upset and gave me the impression that he did not believe my explanation. I went to a physiotherapist and had ultrasound treatment, but I was restricted to easy runs and strides. I must have looked and sounded like an athlete who was seeking an excuse not to run and Pieter was not very sympathetic. But the pain in my leg was real all right and I remain convinced that it was a hamstring strain brought on by that extra, unscheduled session. There were contributing factors if you looked for them: the tartan track in San Diego on which I had trained barefoot was 'thin' and I did my long runs on tar roads. Your legs take a pounding on hard surfaces, particularly if you don't wear shoes, and it may be that the injury would have surfaced anyway. I still think the additional track session uncovered the injury; there was now a hole in my Olympic balloon, although I carried on regardless, doing as much as I could without aggravating the injury.

It was at about this time that Pieter showed me a list of the entrants for the 3,000 metres. I had never heard of the names of some of the athletes and it was weird looking at the semi-final line-up and wondering who they were, what they were like and what tactics they would use. Was I good enough to beat them? Just how good was Puica? And what about Wendy Sly? I had, of course, heard about Puica, but I didn't know nearly enough about her. Was she a front-runner? Did she like to hang back and finish with a devastating burst of speed? It was like looking into a cloudy crystal ball. The images were not clear, just the names, and with hindsight Pieter and I should have done our homework to find out just who my opposition was. There had not been much time for that, though. I was a novice in international terms, the 'wonder girl' born in South Africa who had muscled into the British team with what everybody regarded as almost indecent haste, and I had no idea of what I was up against. The race had been billed as a Decker v Budd showdown, yet few people bothered to consider the credentials of some of the other girls in the race. Mary was the American golden girl and I the pretender to her throne on the basis that I had broken the world 5,000 metres record. Big deal. The 5,000 metres record had been 'soft' and not particularly difficult for any top-class runner to break, but it was enough to set me up as the danger girl in the Los Angeles 3,000 metres and earn for me a reputation as a potential world-beater – a reputation I just did not deserve in view of my inexperience. I was good, certainly a world-class athlete, but did I really have the class to be touted as one of the favourites?

The *Mail*'s idea of publishing Zola Budd's Olympic Games diary led to further strain between Pieter and me. Every day Pieter had to ring the *Mail* with details of what I had done and this would be turned into my 'diary' by faceless 'ghostwriters'. Just another example of the lengths to which the media will go. My real diary was more of a log book, containing details of my training and nothing like the accounts being printed in the newspaper. When I realized how much detail Pieter was feeding the *Mail* I stopped telling him about the more interesting day-to-day happenings in my life: like the time I was doing my laundry at the coin-operated machines and Steve Ovett came in with his wife – my mouth just dropped open at the thought of being in such illustrious company. Here was one of the world's greatest athletes, a giant of a man in middle distance running terms, actually in the same place as me, and I couldn't take my eyes off him. How could a world record holder seem so normal? I felt like a groupie at a rock concert being in the presence of a superstar and, ridiculous as it sounds, I was terribly proud when, noticing that Steve didn't have any washing powder, I offered him mine. That was a moment to savour – Steve Ovett using my powder to wash his clothes!

This was exactly the kind of incident the *Mail* would snap up for the diary, but I didn't tell Pieter about it immediately. I felt dreadful concealing something like this from him, because I didn't want it in the newspaper, but I eventually told Pieter about Steve and he agreed not to pass it on to the *Mail*. Fortunately for me, the diary apparently contravened a ruling that precluded an athlete in my position from 'writing' a regular newspaper column. I breathed a sigh of relief when the silly charade was stopped.

I wasn't the only British athlete looking for grass fields or tracks on which to run. Lots of runners like working on grass and one day British coach Harry Wilson, with whom I was later to have an acrimonious relationship, announced some important news: he knew where there was a patch of grass! It sounded too good to be true because we were all heartily sick and tired of the synthetic training track. We all piled into a car belonging to one of the liaison officers at the holding camp and, with Harry driving and a great grinding of gears, we set off. It was funny watching Harry negotiate the traffic, because he was so short he could barely see over the dashboard. There was a surprise in store when we arrived and saw just how small the patch of grass was, but we made the most of it. We were next to a beach with people all around, but nothing was going to deprive us of this golden opportunity to train on grass – even if we had to run around it about ten times for every kilometre. I stopped after twenty-five minutes because I was tired, but the other British athletes continued tearing around as though their lives depended on it.

Incidents like that brightened up my life no end, and I found everything exciting. The trips we made were a real treat for a girl like me who had led a pretty secluded life in the Free State. It was wonderful going on all the funfair rides at Disney World, where they were celebrating Donald Duck's fiftieth birthday, and I also went to Sea World and watched the killer whales and dolphins. I was still very keen on photography and I must have used rolls and rolls of film as I captured it all for posterity.

Not such fun was a visit to the San Diego Zoo. I love animals and birds, but they were not the focus of attention at the zoo – I was. Another of the *Mail*'s stunts, the object of the exercise was a photographic shoot for a *Mail* photographer whom I disliked. He had a huge nose, and I nicknamed him in Afrikaans, 'the man with a stone in his nose', which was not very kind. But I found his comments intensely annoying as he made me pose this way and that; in the end I felt like one of the monkeys stuck behind bars.

Also huge were some of the women I saw at the holding camp. They were there for a religious congress and they were enormous. In the midst of a group of super-fit athletes they stuck out like a sore thumb and it was obvious they didn't care about being overweight – not the way they tucked into cherry pies and syrup for breakfast. I must admit that as a lover of junk food – many runners are – I over-indulged at the holding camp for the first few days, eating waffles with syrup and chocolate milk before reverting to my usual diet of toast for breakfast.

One memorable day in San Diego saw the arrival of Princess Anne by helicopter. Most of the British contingent shied away from meeting the Princess Royal by deciding that the synthetic track was too hard and that they had to train elsewhere. The place was just about deserted and Fatima Whitbread and I were 'commanded' to be present for a royal audience. I was nervous and luckily Fatima did all the talking but, once again, I was struck by the fact that high-profile people like Ovett in the sporting world and Princess Anne were not much different from us mere mortals. Our royal visitor was very pleasant, asking how we felt and whether we were enjoying ourselves, and I hope she wasn't too disappointed at my showing in the Games.

It wasn't long after meeting the Princess Royal that it was time to go to the Olympic Village at the University of Los Angeles. Nigel Cooper took me there by car and we listened on the radio to the women's marathon. I can remember feeling very proud for Joan Benoit when she won because she deserved it after a good run and I wondered if I would be so lucky. My fantasies ended when we got to the Village and Nigel dropped me off at the gate. This was the real world and I was impressed by the massive security exercise being mounted to protect us from possible terrorist action. Security was tight – there were even helicopters flying above the Village at night – but I got my clearance and moved into an apartment I shared with several other British girls.

In spite of the friction that often flared up between us, I started missing Pieter almost immediately and the loneliness I had felt without him in England set in again. He wasn't allowed inside the Village and my desire to return to South Africa as quickly as possible became overwhelming. In desperation I telephoned my sister Estelle in Bloemfontein: 'I don't care what happens in the Olympics, I just want to go home', I told her. Poor Estelle, it was about 3 a.m. South African time and she did her best to calm me down. I felt a lot better afterwards because it always helps to get things off your chest, to be able to tell somebody close to you how you really feel, and I was in a much better frame of mind the following day.

Inevitably, I had to face the press in Los Angeles and being next in line after that wonderful British decathlete Daley Thompson, I found the men from the media initially quite relaxed. Daley has the gift of the gab and a flair for the unusual, to go with his superb performance in the toughest event of them all; on this occasion it was full value for money. As I heard the story, he was wearing

71

a hat and after being quizzed on his rivalry with German Jurgen Hingsen, whipped it off and, pointing to his bandaged head, said, 'He gives me a headache.'

I wish I could handle the press like that because it was the press who gave *me* a headache. Apart from countless political questions, which were fielded by Nigel Cooper, my press conference seemed like a pilot for the 'Mary and Zola Show'. The other athletes didn't get a mention in what the press had already decided would be a two-woman race: it was all Mary and me. What did I think about Mary? Was it true I had her picture on my wall? Could I beat her? All the media hype was encapsulated by an episode that took place outside the interview room when Pieter and I were having lunch. I ordered a turkey sandwich and Pieter a huge, colourful salad. 'Oh no,' said the *Mail* men, 'the salad will make a better picture, so please swop dishes.' Although I had not even ordered it, I posed with it for a photograph that was to be published everywhere, along with inane captions along the lines of 'We hope Zola didn't eat all of that.'

People accuse me of not wanting to talk to the press, but can I be blamed when I got off to such a difficult start? One publicity stunt after another finally takes its toll and I was overpowered by all the attention at a time when I was feeling very unsure of myself. The Olympic Games were hardly the ideal place for a young girl to make her real international début and putting me under the spotlight suited everybody else in the 3,000 metres field. Mary was an old hand who had learnt to handle the publicity and, although I didn't realize it then, Maricica Puica would be happy to let her legs and lungs do the talking. Feeling my way around the English language like a blind person in an unfamiliar room, I was at a distinct disadvantage. I was taking all the pressure while my British teammate, Wendy Sly, was comfortably out of the limelight. Nobody expected much from her in the 3,000 metres final.

8
The Fall

I was really nervous before the 3,000 metres heats on the evening of 8 August 1984, because this was the big one, the Olympic Games. I had sacrificed everything to be here and now it was up to me to produce the goods, to make all the trauma of the previous four months worthwhile. We warmed up at the University of San Diego and caught a bus to the stadium where we went to another, much smaller, warm-up area. The first thing that struck me then was the strength and power of Maricica Puica. She seemed so big, not in physical size but in overall stature and presence, almost larger than life in a way, and I knew I would have a fight on my hands if I qualified for the final.

To reach the stadium from the warm-up area we had to walk down a long, dark passage and my first impression of the stadium was of all the lights and the huge video screen. I couldn't stop looking around me and at all the people as I made my way to the start, but I blocked it out at the gun and ran into the lead. I didn't really run hard because I didn't have to and when I looked behind me I knew I would easily qualify for the final. Puica came past me like a steam engine in the last 200 metres to clock 8:43.32, but that was her style and I was content to finish third in 8:44.62. It was, in a way, a lazy run for me. The final was the race that really counted and once I was on the track and running in the heat, I can remember thinking: 'Nine minutes, please pass quickly.' I told Pieter about the laziness, but he said I shouldn't worry: 'It's OK,' he said, 'after hard training and a lay-off of a couple of days it's perfectly normal to feel that way. It means you will be all right in the final.'

The final was late on a warm afternoon and it was a long drive in the bus to the warm-up area. Because it was so hot I took a huge plastic bottle full of soft drink with me and I kept having sips on the bus. I was too nervous to hold a proper conversation with any of the other athletes, although I did chat to an athlete from Swaziland and a diver from Zimbabwe, and I felt strangely tired when we arrived at the warm-up area. There was a room with beds in it where we could relax before loosening up, but I was too tense to sleep. My British teammate, Wendy Sly, was, on the other hand, remarkably cool. She had no trouble having a snooze and I ended up reading a cowboy novel in an attempt to keep my mind off the race.

Perhaps it was nerves, but I couldn't understand why I felt so tired. 'I'll never be able to run properly like this', I thought as I went to warm up with my legs feeling like lead. How, I wondered, would I be able to beat Mary? She looked great as she did all her exercises in a red outfit while I felt horrible as all I could do were a few strides because the injury was hurting. I could run, but I couldn't stretch properly and I was really glad to see a friendly face when Pieter arrived at the warm-up area after getting a special pass.

It sounds incredible, but Pieter and I never talked tactics before the final. We knew Mary was a front-runner and I think we both assumed I would go out there and try to hang on. I could feel the pressure from Pieter, who was expecting me to do well, and it reminded me of the time I came second in the South African 10 kilometres championships in 1981. On that occasion I was beaten by Diane

74

Massyn and Pieter was so disappointed that he wouldn't talk to me afterwards. He only relented when a friend of his said it would be a good idea to congratulate me.

In Los Angeles, I knew I was good, perhaps good enough to run a place, but I knew deep down in my heart that I wasn't strong enough to win an Olympic final at that early stage of my international career. That was the wrong attitude and I made the mistake of going into the final with an overwhelming feeling of 'Get it over' instead of 'Run hard'. I couldn't help it but, looking back, I think I realized that once the Olympics were over the *Mail* would be out of my life and I would be able to start everything all over again. I was still young and I had plenty of time to rebuild a career that had been turned upside-down by the trauma of the preceding months. In spite of all the training, I wanted only to get it all over with; and, apart from Mary, I did not even know who my opponents really were. Mary was the only one who counted and we never considered Maricica Puica or Wendy Sly.

The one bright spot on a day that was to shake the athletics world came when the athletes in the 3,000 metres final had to show their running shoes to an official, whose task it was to see that the spikes conformed to specifications. I was barefoot, so I just picked up my feet and showed them to him, white plasters on my toes and all. The poor man nearly cracked up laughing, but what else could I have done? Everybody else had spikes and I had to show him something . . .

The worst thing before the final was the crowd. They kept chanting 'Mary, Mary' and it was horrible. They were so biased and they made it look as though the final was only between me and Mary. It made me feel guilty, because I worried about how the other runners in the race were reacting. The crowd made it seem as though they didn't count – which, with hindsight, was probably the best thing that could have happened to them. With the race billed as a Decker v Budd showdown, nobody was expecting much from the others, so they had the advantage of facing the starter without any pressure.

After the gun I followed Mary and stayed as close as possible to the front group. Mary went off like a bolt of lightning and I thought: 'My goodness, this is fast. I hope they don't carry on like this.' Fortunately, the pace slowed in the middle of the race, and it was the bunching as we all came together that contributed to Mary's fall with three laps to run.

The stage was set for disaster when Mary, who was in the lead with me outside her and Puica behind, slowed down. But the most important figure, one who was virtually ignored in the endless post mortems afterwards, was Wendy, looming up on my outside and starting to box me in.

I could feel her bumping my arm as she raced into contention and I had three choices: take the lead, drop back, or run wide. I couldn't get behind Mary because Puica was there and I couldn't go outside because Wendy was there, coming closer all the time and crowding me, bumping my arm. The only place left was the front, so I started accelerating to get out of trouble. Mary didn't respond immediately to my change of pace and when I saw she wasn't coming with me as I picked up the pace I cut inside. There was still a bit of bumping – Wendy was moving in – but I didn't see Mary's fall and my conscience is clear. As far as I could see, the inside lane was open because I was overtaking Mary and I wouldn't have moved across the track if it hadn't been clear. I almost fell, but I didn't know if it was Mary, Wendy or Puica who bumped me. With Wendy coming closer it was a case of either going to the front or losing a place and another lap went by before I realized that something was terribly wrong.

Puica had, at that stage, already taken the lead, suddenly shooting past me with a tremendous surge. I can remember thinking, 'Oh my, what's happening now?' as I tried to keep in touch and when next I looked around I saw that the field

76

had opened up. 'Who's missing?' I wondered as I ran hard to keep up. 'Somebody must have fallen.'

But who had gone? When did it happen? I looked again and knew intuitively that Mary had gone. What I didn't know was that it was me that she had tangled with before sprawling on to the inside of the track, ruining forever her dreams and those of millions of Americans of that elusive gold medal. The booing of the crowd on the penultimate lap told me that Mary had fallen and that because I had been closest to Mary I must have been involved. It took a while after the bumping for me to realize what had happened and I could feel the antagonism of the crowd.

Can you imagine what it's like to have 90,000 people booing at you? It was awful and in that instant all that mattered to me was getting as far away from them as possible. Pieter had drummed into me from the time I first joined his training squad that you never stop in a race, ever, no matter what happens. Well, Mary had fallen and it looked like my fault, but I had to finish the race. What I couldn't endure, however, was the thought of facing all those people on the rostrum. It sounds easy to say, but I knew once the race had started that I was good enough to win a silver or bronze medal. Deep inside me, though, was now a dread of standing on a rostrum and I began running slower and slower. People passed me and I didn't care – everything had collapsed and I just wanted out – I almost walked across the finish line.

The race over, the only person I looked for was my friend Cornelia Burki. She walked with me away from the track and when I saw a distraught Mary in the tunnel leading out of the stadium I told her I was sorry. I felt even worse when she looked up at me and snarled, 'Don't bother!'

9
Great Escape

Even now, when I look back at that race, I get the feeling that it was all so unfair. After the turmoil of the previous four months, the emotional upheaval with my father and coach, and the fact that I was really a reluctant Olympian anyway who had had grave reservations about going to Los Angeles in the first place, why did it have to be me who tangled with Mary? It could have been Mary and Puica or Mary and Wendy. It could also have been Wendy and Puica. So why me? Why the girl who at the beginning of 1984 did not even expect to be facing the starter in Los Angeles? I had been thrown to the lions in the Colosseum and now wanted to escape with the minimum of scarring.

I can understand Mary's anger when she uttered those two fateful words. 'Don't bother!' was a cry of frustration because she, too, had been given a chance of attaining Olympic glory, only to have it snatched away. Mary had always been an athlete I respected for her great ability and competitive edge and had I been in her position I might have reacted in the same way.

Although secure in the knowledge that I was not guilty of any 'crime' during the 3,000 metres final, it took a long time to come to terms with what had happened and I hated the thought that so many people held me responsible for the fall. But my conscience was cleared completely when I received this letter from Mary, dated 2 December 1984:

Dear Zola,
I've been wanting to write this letter to you for a long time. The reason I haven't sent this letter before is because I was sure that you would not receive it personally.

I simply want to apologize to you for hurting your feelings at the Olympics. There are many reasons that people react the way they do at certain times in their lives and I'm sure you understand that that was a very difficult time for me.

I'm sorry I turned you away after the race, it was a very hard moment for me emotionally and I reacted in an emotional manner.

I know that we do not know each other personally, but the next time we meet I would like to shake your hand and let everything that has happened be put behind us. Who knows; sometimes even the fiercest competitors become friends.

Good luck in Phoenix, I hope you are fit and healthy and I am looking forward to competing with you this summer.

Yours in sport,
(signed) Mary Decker

What a sporting gesture! It helped make up for the agony of the moment when all I wanted to do after Mary's rebuff in Los Angeles was get as far away from the stadium as possible. It didn't help when some of the other athletes who had been in the race told me not to worry, that it wasn't my fault. I wanted out, the sooner the better, and I collected my clothes, got dressed and headed for the area where we caught the buses as quickly as I could.

On my way to the bus I saw Wendy, who couldn't believe that she had won the silver medal. I congratulated her and even then I was able to share in her triumph. At least someone had got something out of what had, for me, been a nightmare, and I was glad for Wendy because she had been running badly all season. When the bus came, I got on with Pam Pierce and a black woman athlete whom I didn't know for the longest drive ever back to the Olympic Village. I was still numb with shock and all I wanted was to get away from everything connected with the Games. I was deeply moved when I realised that I had the sympathy of the black athlete, the only other passenger on the bus apart from Pam and me. She was aware of the incident, she saw how unhappy I was and she was crying.

Back at the Village, I packed immediately and then went to see the British officials to arrange for Pieter to collect me. While I was waiting Seb Coe came in and he was very philosophical about coming second in the 800 metres final. I couldn't understand how he could be so cool, calm and collected when he still had the 1,500 metres to run. I was anything but calm and, helped by Pam Pierce and Mary Peters, carried my luggage to the car where my coach was waiting. Pieter wanted to get out and greet the British officials, but I was in such a hurry to leave I wouldn't let him. 'Get in the car,' I said impatiently. 'I want to go.'

I sought refuge in my mother's flat and attempted to blot out the Games. In a symbolic act of defiance the following day, I took a pair of running shoes and threw them in the dustbin. 'I'm never going to run again', I told myself. 'I'm never going to run again in my whole life.' It helped relieve the tension . . . and I knew all the time in the back of my mind that I had another pair of shoes in my suitcase!

All I did in Los Angeles after the fall was eat ice cream (lots of it), watch TV and go to the pool. I gained some consolation from that great New Zealand miler, John Walker, whom I met when I went down for a swim. 'Don't worry, Zola,' he said with an understanding smile, 'it wasn't your fault.' I really appreciated his kindness and was again pleasantly surprised when I read a balanced account of the episode in a local newspaper which had somehow resisted the temptation to lay the blame on me for sending their golden girl sprawling. Many other newspapers, though, made the most of my misfortune; and a 'brilliant' idea by ABC television was responsible for me standing up to Pieter for the first time in our relationship.

ABC wanted to film a debate between me and Mary, and Pieter thought it would be a good idea. 'It will settle everything', he said, but I wasn't having any of it. My answer was a flat 'No', and it upset Pieter dreadfully. 'Why not?' he asked. 'You can get your point across.' What Pieter didn't realize was that I was not yet proficient in English. Afrikaans is my first language and I was still learning how to speak English correctly. My English was definitely not good enough for me to attack or to defend myself effectively in open debate; and Mary was so experienced in handling the media that she would have made mincemeat out of me. I wanted a fair hearing and I wasn't going to get it on a live television show.

Pieter was very angry when I turned the ABC offer down and I felt awful going against his wishes. I had never stood up to him before and it was hard to say 'No' to a man who had been banking on me winning a medal. I was lucky to have Ma with me in Los Angeles, because Pieter wasn't much help as I tried to block out the memory of 90,000 people booing me. Pieter and Carin were not getting on very well at the time and Pieter was so disillusioned that he no longer seemed to have the strength to give me any encouragement. He was busy trying to get himself back into shape after the let-down and he acted as though I had deprived him of something. I felt I had disappointed him terribly when I saw his long face, which seemed to be saying, 'I gave up everything for you, even my job, to move to England to be with you – and look what happened.' While a medal would have been a just reward for his devotion, I think Pieter had the idea that it would also have given me the spur I needed to stay in England instead of returning to South Africa. That was, however, academic and in the absence of any real support from my coach, I was fortunate to have Ma to fall back on.

'I'm sorry about what happened,' she said after the race. 'Just remember that I will always love you, no matter what happens.' I was so embarrassed about being at the centre of another controversy that I didn't want to see anyone – and Ma rallied round. She put on a brave face and tried to make me feel better by giving me love, making my favourite food and feeding me ice cream. I don't know what I would have done without her because I was totally deflated. It felt as though my whole life had collapsed, for at that stage of my career running was everything to me. My athletics took up ninety-nine per cent of my time and it seemed to me that I would have to start from scratch again. After all the publicity over my selection for Britain, I was drained – my dreams lay in tatters and I no longer had the inclination to train or plan a strategy. I needed somebody to care for me as Zola, not me as an athlete, and Ma was wonderful. 'Time to sleep, Zola . . . time to eat. Isn't it time you did your washing? . . . Do you want to watch television?' There is nothing like a mother's love and Ma made me feel wanted when I felt like an outcast.

I still didn't want to see anyone else, not even Pieter, and like a child reaching for a favourite doll, I longed for my pets. My dog, Fraaier, was a special favourite and the most important thing for me then was to see her. 'I want Fraaier,' I told myself. 'I want to be with Fraaier on the farm in Bloemfontein, I don't want anyone else . . .'

We left for London after two days and it was two days too many as far as I was concerned. It was quite exciting to be driven to the airport by police car and they treated us like real VIPs by taking us right up to the steps of the jumbo jet. John Bryant was with us and I told him that I wanted to leave for South Africa as soon as possible. Luckily, we had our tickets with us and as soon as we got to London we booked a flight straight to Jan Smuts airport in Johannesburg.

I was in England for just two days before going to South Africa and I was so excited about going 'home' that I hardly slept. 'It's all over,' I thought. 'We're on the way.' I was still staying with Pieter and Carin and we had our hands full packing boxes while Pieter slept. They had loads of stuff to pack and we bought takeaway food to avoid having to unpack any kitchen utensils. Like me, Ma was in a seventh heaven because we were going home, but my father was staying on. I had not seen Daddy since walking out of the house before the Games, and I visited him in an attempt to patch everything up between us. I had got him a pen and lighter in America, but I shouldn't have bothered. While I thought that all would be forgiven now that the Games were out of the way, Daddy had other ideas. 'Oh, I'm glad you still remember me', he said sarcastically when I walked into the living-room to give him my gift. I was stunned at his reaction and just walked away. If he wouldn't bother, I wouldn't bother – and the rift between us widened.

Although I was very disturbed by the split between Daddy and me, there was an element of wry humour in our departure. John Bryant came to fetch us with two cars, and just when we thought we had loaded everything, we realized that there were still some boxes in the house. 'My fondue pot,' said Carin as she ran into the house, 'I must get my fondue pot.' I couldn't believe what I was hearing. It was the fondue at Pieter's house that had forced me to choose between Pieter and Daddy before the Olympics and I thought, 'Oh no, not the fondue pot! How can you take that?'

But fetch it she did and we headed for the airport with Pieter driving as though his life depended on it. We were

83

in an old blue Vauxhall which the *Mail* had given him and Pieter was going so fast that John could hardly keep up in the second car. My last impression of England was John Bryant of the *Mail* and his family waving goodbye in Terminal Three at Heathrow airport. I couldn't wait to get on to the plane and Ma was delighted. She drank champagne during the flight while I thought about Fraaier. I was desperate to get back to everything that was dear to me – the rest of my family and my pets – and athletics was the last thing on my mind.

10
Demo Nightmare

Returning to the land of my birth after the Olympic Games was a strange experience for me. I had longed so desperately to get back to familiar surroundings and now that the time had arrived I felt nervous and even a little hesitant. I had changed in the few months I had been away, become a different person in many respects, and never having been in the position of coming back to South Africa after a trip abroad before, I didn't quite know what to expect.

Uncertain in the aircraft about how I would feel after we touched down, I could hardly wait for the door to be opened at Johannesburg's Jan Smuts airport and I was thrilled to see that everything was just as I remembered it. South Africa is a land of wide open spaces, and there's plenty of that at Jan Smuts. I could see for miles and my spirits soared as I took in the smoky blue sky on a day that was halfway between summer and winter, the pale brown grass that would only turn green during the rains, and the smell of Africa. This was the countryside I was used to, not the grey skies and dampness of England, and I looked around me in fascination on the way to the terminal buildings.

The customs officials were friendly and Ma and I quickly got the formalities over with before going into the arrival hall, where we were met by Quintus. We were also greeted by a frenzied mob of pressmen, but we walked straight through them. Even if I had felt like giving an interview, which I certainly did not, I would have been unable to say anything because I was still contracted to the *Mail* and it was great not having to worry about another round of questions. Priority number one for me was getting to Bloemfontein with the minimum of delay, and we only made one stop, at Parys, where the people in the cafe recognized me and gave me food and a cool drink on the house.

'Welcome home Zola', said the banner that greeted me at the farm as we drove in, trailed by journalists from Bloemfontein's *Volksblad* newspaper, who had 'ambushed' us about 50 kilometres from the city and given us an unofficial escort. It was wonderful to be home, and the photographer had to wait for his pictures as I went straight into the house to see my beloved animals. There was Fraaier, looking like an American football player after having all the hair on her rump shaved off so that she could have a hip operation. I was so pleased to see her, but couldn't help laughing at the way she looked with thick hair on the front of her body and an almost bald behind. 'My poor dog,' I thought as I petted her, 'I've waited such a long time to see you again.' After paying my respects to Fraaier, I went to find the cats. Johnny had by this time been shipped back to South Africa and she seemed pleased to see me, as did Stompie.

The important business done, I was happy to pose for pictures before settling back into my old routine at the farm. Although I had only been away for five months, everything seemed to take on a different quality. Objects I had taken for granted now took on new significance, like the pot plants and photographs and pictures on the wall. Mary Decker's photograph was still on the wall, and that's one of the first things that changed – it came down very quickly.

The next few days were difficult, with the press at the gate all day long looking for that exclusive interview or special picture. They didn't give me the freedom I craved to wander around the farm and be myself, so Ma resorted to a little trickery to throw the newshounds off the scent. One day she put a suitcase in the back of the car, threw a blanket over it and drove out past the waiting pressmen. 'Ah ha,' they thought, 'she's trying to sneak Zola away, but she won't get away from us.' They jumped into their cars to follow my mother, and I was left in peace to walk where I pleased on the farm, renewing my acquaintance with all the animals.

There were, however, serious matters to discuss, and at the top of the list was my father and his relationship with Ma and me. Ma wanted a divorce, and a few weeks after my return and before my father came back, the subject came up over Sunday lunch. Quintus was hurt and upset over the rift in the family and confused by my attitude to Daddy. He couldn't understand my antagonism and did not think that I was being fair to our father by walking out of his life and wanting nothing further to do with him. But Quintus, loving and loyal to his father, had no idea of what I had gone through in England with Daddy and, consequently, could not understand my attitude. According to Quintus, my coach, Pieter, was the person to blame for the split. Pieter had forced me to choose between him and Daddy and it was Pieter's fault that I had walked out. Now that just wasn't true and I defended Pieter, telling Quintus bluntly that if Daddy had interferred in his life the same way he had in mine he would feel the same way as I did. With that I stormed off to my room and had a good cry, mortified that my brother had no real perception of what I had gone through. Eventually, two years later, I would relent and agree with Quintus to attempt a reconciliation between my parents; but it was no good and they divorced on 18 November 1986.

My father, who had stayed on in England, came home

in late October and the day he got back I moved out of the house. I had been prepared for his return and had already rented a small flat and transferred my belongings, so it wasn't a problem for me. He had hurt me too much in England for me to keep our relationship cordial and I refused to greet him if I saw him while I was visiting Ma. One day when I was spending time with Ma my father came in, full of bravado, produced a measuring tape and began sizing up the garage. His relationship with my mother had also deteriorated beyond repair and he, too, was moving out – into the garage. Within a week my father had converted the garage into a flat and when he moved in I moved back into the house. Well, sort of: I still kept the flat, but felt much more comfortable with Ma, so I spent most evenings with her, often sleeping over. It was awkward, though, and very strained when Daddy and I did set eyes on each other, and it was bizarre sitting in the house and listening to him coughing at night.

In spite of the fact that Elizna van Zyl and I had had our differences when she came to England to be with me and ended up taking my father's side, she remained a true friend. One night when I was to sleep in the flat and she was visiting, she told me that it was wrong for me to be on my own. 'Come to my place,' she said. 'You can't stay here by yourself.' That was an act of kindness on her part and one that I really appreciated. It proved the value of friendship, something I have not always been lucky to experience with my unsettled lifestyle, and I was glad that there were people on whom I could count.

My desire to run was still strong and it was inevitable that I should start training again soon after my return and that the subject of my fledgling international career should be under close scrutiny in the media. I was back with Pieter's old squad and enjoying running with all my friends, and at first Pieter didn't push the subject because he knew how I felt. The first clash came after I had gone for the test to get my driver's licence. Before leaving for England I had won a Citi Golf for winning the 5,000 metres at the Volkswagen Prestige meeting in Port Elizabeth but had not been able to collect it. The organizers kept the car for me while I was away and now that I was back there was to be a ceremony when they handed me the keys. Feeling terribly independent after my overseas adventure, I decided that I would drive the car away myself, but first I had to get my licence.

That was quite funny because during my test I couldn't manage the parallel parking. After a couple of botched attempts by me to get into the parking bay, the traffic officer, who would have been within his rights to fail me, took pity, got out of the car, and directed me safely in. Very pleased with myself, I went to the ceremonial handing-over of the keys and when asked by the press at the ceremony if I intended competing overseas, replied, 'I don't know'.

When Pieter heard my answer, our row started all over again. 'How can you say that?' he asked. 'You must tell them you are going back.' Well, I didn't want to go, and Pieter seemed to accept my decision. 'OK,' he said during a telephone conversation, 'you can stay in South Africa and I will arrange everything so you don't have any problems.' Great, I thought, that's what I've been waiting to hear. From being so positive, however, Pieter soon changed his mind and we kicked the overseas idea around as though it were a football. In the end we reached a compromise: 'If you really want to live in South Africa, you must contact the South African Amateur Athletic Union and ask them if you can compete here again', he said. Anxious not to lose my advantage, I rang SAAAU president Professor Charles Nieuwoudt and arranged a meeting in Pretoria. It went well, the SAAAU would be happy to have me back, and Pieter began planning my South African 'comeback'.

It was done through Jannie Momberg, a vice-president of the SAAAU and chairman of the Western Province AAA, whom I had got to know well during my career in South Africa. A wealthy wine farmer, Jannie owned the beautiful Neethlingshof estate and I had often stayed at his home when I competed at the Coetzenburg Stadium in Stellenbosch. His wife, Trienie, was always very kind to me and I got along well with the Momberg boys, Jannie and Altus. Jannie senior was a kindly man, given to verbosity and sometimes overpowering, but he loved athletics and had always taken a keen interest in my progress.

A Dream Mile meeting was scheduled for Coetzenburg on 10 November 1984 and knowing that I wanted to run in South Africa again, Jannie came to Bloemfontein. He was keen for me to compete at Coetzenburg, where he would put on a special 3,000 metres race for me, and after he talked to Pieter the three of us had a meeting at the Holiday Inn, where Jannie agreed to pay me around 2,000 South African rands in appearance money if I ran the first race of my South African comeback in Stellenbosch. It was also agreed that I would go to Stellenbosch a week prior to the Dream Mile meeting so as not to draw attention to myself by arriving in the Cape the day before the race.

This, however, presented a problem because I was in Stellenbosch at the time of an annual dinner in Bloemfontein at which the province's sportsman and woman of the year were to be named. I was to get the women's award but, being in the Cape where I was training for the 3,000 metres, I couldn't attend the banquet and somebody else received the accolade. But my absence was noted and the Free State athletics officials became suspicious. If I was to run in South Africa again they wanted it to be on my 'home' territory on Bloemfontein, not Stellenbosch, and news of the race buzzed through the higher echelons of South African athletics. With the Free State putting the pressure on, Jannie abruptly changed his mind. From being excited and positive about the race one day, he was dead against it the next and I was left with the impression that his about turn was prompted by the realization that he would be left to carry the can for ending my international career by encouraging me to run in South Africa.

90

Jannie's view now was that as a British athlete I should make the most of my opportunity to run internationally, and he planned accordingly. John Bryant had already been to Stellenbosch to confer with Jannie and so, too, had British Amateur Athletic Board secretary Nigel Cooper. They both wanted me back overseas and the solution to their predicament came from Western Province rugby coach Dawie Snyman. An astute coach who takes a lively interest in the whole sporting spectrum, Snyman rang Jannie and suggested a 'come and go' situation. Let me compete internationally, argued Snyman, and spend time in South Africa. That way I might settle down.

The idea had merit and I agreed to the compromise, with the proviso that I should have the chance to study for a degree by correspondence through the University of South Africa (Unisa). Money was a stumbling-block, though, because most of what I had received was held by my father, and it was here that another wine farmer and industrialist, Graham Boonzaier, became part of my life. I remember meeting Graham for the first time when this man with black hair and a black beard arrived at Neethlingshof in a Toyota landcruiser. He offered to provide the bridging finance which enabled me to shuttle between South Africa and England with Pieter and he suggested the formation of the Zola Budd Trust, which would handle my affairs. Graham also put up the money to cover the expenses incurred by Pieter and my friends who would periodically travel to England to train with me and give me the companionship a lonely girl needed in England.

The Zola Budd Sports Trust was formed on 19 November 1984 and although I was to contest it later, it appointed Jannie, Pieter and Graham as my sole representatives for a period of four years. The agreement read in part: 'I appoint the aforesaid persons jointly to represent me generally in regard to all matters relating to and concerning my athletics career and to negotiate and conclude all contracts on my behalf. This appointment is made on the basis that my

91

said representatives will at all times be acting in close co-operating [sic] with the British Amateur Athletics Board.'

After I had agreed to the compromise of training in South Africa and racing in England, I moved to Stellenbosch at Jannie's instigation. It seemed to me that he was anxious to get me away from my family – especially my mother, whom he regarded as a negative influence – and, anyway, Pieter had also gone to Stellenbosch.

With all systems go Jannie, who by now had the confidence of the British Amateur Athletic Board and their blessing for the plan for me to 'come and go', set about arranging a race for me overseas. It's ironic that in 1984 the British Board was prepared to countenance my living in South Africa and racing overseas, but its complicity in an arrangement that was to give my opponents all the ammunition they needed to shoot me down is clear.

In a letter to Jannie and Trienie, dated 13 November and written on a BAAB letterhead, general secretary Nigel Cooper had this to say:

It was marvellously kind of you both to take so much time and care to make my short visit to South Africa so comfortable and enjoyable. As to Cape Province, I can but repeat what Sir Walter Raleigh said those centuries ago, 'the fayrest Cape in all the world'.

Twas good to see Zola smilingly enjoying herself, due principally to being on the farm with yourselves. Only time will show whether or not she will decide to compete internationally once more. To that end I hope the discussions between yourself and Graham prove productive.

I have taken the liberty to have my publishers send copies of our recent athletics publications to you in the hope there might be a small market in the Republic!?!

92

Well, the discussions were productive, I agreed to the arrangement, and the British board wasted no time in giving me the green light. In a letter dated 21 November 1984, addressed to me at Neethlingshof, copied to Jannie and signed by Nigel Cooper, I received the good news:

> Permission is hereby granted for you to compete in a road race in Zurich on 30th December 1984.
>   Please accept our good wishes for a most enjoyable and successful visit to Switzerland.

So, I had taken the big step and gone along with Jannie's wishes, although I was still torn apart inside. Jannie's boast was always that 'a happy Budd will beat the world', but there were times right at the start of our relationship when I wasn't happy. I was still trying to come to grips with the idea of running overseas, and my training wasn't going well. Jannie tried to inspire me by taking me into Stellenbosch by car and leaving me to run home to the estate, and he was keen for me to race at least once overseas before making a decision on my future. 'Run in Zurich,' he urged me. 'After that you can make up your mind. It won't be anything like as bad as the Olympics.'

With everything agreed, I went back to Bloemfontein to put the finishing touches to my preparations for the 8-kilometres race in Zurich. But I was still assailed by doubts over the wisdom of my decision and it affected my training. When the morning of my departure arrived I was desperately casting around for an excuse not to go and I didn't even bother to pack. Scheduled to meet Pieter for a final training session at Loch Logan, I drove away before he arrived and at my mother's house I found some sleeping pills which I thought would do the trick. I gulped

93

some down thinking that if they knocked me out nobody would be able to wake me up and I would miss the flight. No such luck. I was still wide awake and finally followed the advice of my sister Cara, who urged me to 'give it a go'.

In much the same frame of mind as I was in before the Olympics, I flew to Switzerland, adamant that I would get this race over and then return to South Africa as quickly as possible. In our party were Graham, Jannie, Pieter and Carin, and the Swiss gave us real VIP treatment on our arrival. I won the race on 30 December in 26:27 and, with everybody ecstatic over my success, we went to Lech in Austria for a two-day holiday in the snow over the New Year. But I was in no mood for celebrating. Still down in the dumps, I attended a meeting in Jannie's hotel room, where I saw hope reflected on the faces of Jannie, Graham and Pieter. Bucked up by my victory in Zurich over Cornelia Burki, I'm sure they expected a change of heart on my part and they popped the million-dollar question: 'Zola, do you want to continue your international career?'

'No', I said, and their faces dropped in shock. 'Not again', I could see them thinking. 'What's it going to take to bring her round?' The answer was simple: take me back to South Africa. I left Jannie's room and returned to my own, where I cried my eyes out during one of the loneliest nights I can remember. But, like a ball attached to a racket by a piece of elastic, I came back to their way of thinking primarily, I suppose, because I actually believed Pieter when he said I would end up as a nobody on a farm with my mother if I didn't take my chances.

We flew back to London where Jannie arranged a press conference at which a statement written on my behalf was released to the British Press. I knew that Jannie was to meet the media, but I was not informed beforehand of the contents of the statement dated 3 January 1985, which read:

1. I intend to continue my athletics career as a British athlete and intend returning to England during the third week of January 1985.
2. I intend living in Guildford with friends.
3. As 1985 will be a relatively quiet year as far as world meetings are concerned, we will be looking at all aspects of athletics.
4. I will run in the 1,500 metres in the British Indoor championships at Cosford, on January 25 and 26 and, if selected, in the international meeting against the Federal Republic of Germany, also at Cosford, on February 9 1985.
6. I hope to enter for the National Cross Country Championships at Birkenhead on February 16, 1985, but will only decide on competing after determining my fitness for cross country running.
7. I have been invited to run in a 10 kilometres road race in Phoenix, Arizona in the USA as I am keen to experiment with the road running scene in the USA. I will seriously contemplate accepting pending negotiations with the organizers. My decision will be announced shortly.
8. After the USA I will return to South Africa to spend some time with my family and train at an altitude to which I am accustomed before returning to England for the European track season in June.
9. My future career and business/financial matters will be handled through my UK-based trust and administered by a senior member from the London Office of the leading firm of accountants Touche Ross International. This person will also act as my nominated trustee to the BAAB.

My friend and coach of many years, Mr Pieter Labuschagne, will continue with my full training programme. He will also be working in close co-operation regarding athletic matters with Mr Les Jones, Chairman of the International Committee of the BAAB, to help guide my career.

10. I would like to take this special opportunity to publicly thank my friends 'Uncle' Jannie Momberg and 'Uncle' Graham Boonzaier for all they have done to advise, guide and steer me through my difficult times of 1984. It was their love, care and understanding and many hours of just sitting and talking which enabled me to make today's decision.

I realize that things are somewhat changing here from today and I am sure and hope I can still rely on their friendship and interest for many years to come as my career develops to its full potential.

To my coach and friend Mr Pieter Labuschagne and his wife Carin a great thank you to both of you for all you have done for me up to now and I am sure we can build from here today.

11. My final wish is to be treated and accepted as any other British athlete.

Back in Stellenbosch to prepare for the indoor races, I was dreadfully lonely in the posh flat Jannie had arranged for me. It was nice as flats go, but a far cry from the farm in Stellenbosch and the worst thing was that I had no other interests apart from my running. It felt sometimes as though I was going to go mad and I went to a petshop and bought a hamster – just to have something alive in the flat. I called him Hamstring, which I thought was an appropriate name for a runner's rodent, and it was a relief to go overseas again for the indoor meetings.

Reasonably fit, I won the British indoor 1,500 metres championship in 4:11.20 at Cosford on 26 January and the international 3,000 metres race also at Cosford on 9 February in 8:56.1, squashing the Southern Counties women's cross-country championships at Ipswich in between. I won the 5.7 kilometres cross-country in 18:55 after electing to run barefoot against opposition from Pieter and Mel Batty, who both wanted me to wear spikes. I had tried a few strides wearing the spikes, but didn't feel comfortable and took them off, which must have left Mel wondering just why Brooks had signed me up in the first place!

As usual, I wasn't enjoying the weather in England, and I hated training in the snow. It was so foreign to anything I had encountered before, and on occasion Pieter must have despaired of getting any decent performances out of me as I stubbornly refused to train properly. It was snowing when we arrived in Liverpool the day before the British cross-country championships and I wondered how I would cope with the biting cold. The last cross-country I had run in South Africa had been held in searing heat, but on race day in Liverpool on 16 February I actually felt quite good.

I warmed up around the corner from the start; and, although I had been warned to expect trouble, had not anticipated the rabid reception that awaited me from the anti-apartheid demonstrators. There was a huge crowd, people shouting and shoving and mounted police trying to keep the peace. 'Oh no,' I thought. 'How can I run in such a chaotic setting? What's going to happen now?' The sight of the demonstrators and their antagonism frightened me, but, at the same time, I felt acutely embarrassed. What about the other athletes? A situation like this was the last thing they wanted with places in the England team up for grabs, and surely they had the right to compete without being subjected to additional aggravation. I knew that my presence at the race was the cause of all the trouble; it was yet another symptom of the 'Budd syndrome' that faced me overseas – while most athletes had only to arrive at a venue and run, I had first to fight a political fight in which I had no interest and where I was at an immediate disadvantage.

At the gun I ran wide and Angela Tooby opened up a small gap on the first lap; but, as we came to the halfway, the demonstrators suddenly invaded the course. It was like a bad dream and, in spite of the drama of the occasion, I can remember thinking that the protestors resembled characters from a nightmare. They seemed so ugly that I couldn't distinguish males from females and I knew that I could not finish the race. I careered off the course and, with the crowd surrounding me, threatening to suffocate me, I crashed through the bushes, crying, in an attempt to escape. They were tears of frustration for not being permitted to run the race and hopelessness at my situation. 'Take me away from here,' was my silent plea. 'Take me home to Fraaier.' My dog was on my mind the whole time as I stumbled to the car to get dressed and I was feeling sorry for myself when I went to hospital for a precautionary tetanus injection after cutting my legs on the bushes.

Apart from the injustice of it all, the thing that really annoyed me about the entire incident was the fact that I can't recall anybody saying publicly that it had been wrong for the demonstrators to disrupt the race. In a free society demonstrators have every right to protest and I agree with freedom of speech and association. If people want to demonstrate, let them do so, but it should be done peacefully and without impinging on the rights of other individuals. I had the right to finish that race, just as they had the right to protest against my presence, but the demonstrators at Liverpool were no better than the hooligans who have ruined the image of English soccer abroad by their loutish behaviour. It didn't say much for the anti-apartheid lobby in England that it was prepared to sanction actions which affected the performances of athletes other than myself and it was an indication of just how low it was prepared to stoop in its attempts to force me out of Britain.

Not having finished the race, I was fortunate to be pre-selected for the British team to compete in the world cross-country championships in Lisbon and I headed back to South Africa again to train with the sun on my back. Before Lisbon, though, I had the 10-kilometres Continental Homes road race in Phoenix on 2 March and I was startled by the amount of money Graham negotiated for me to take part.

As a businessman, Graham got down to some hard bargaining and I felt guilty for getting $20,000 in appearance money. I was also uncomfortable by the way my race against Wendy Sly was commercialized. My name or face was everywhere, from tee-shirts to posters, and it made me feel cheap and exploited. Buy this Budd souvenir, buy that one; it seemed as though my very soul was up for sale. In the race I ran second to Wendy, in 32:20 to her 32:04 – not a bad effort if the reaction of the people close to me was anything to go by, but I was glad when it was over and I could return to South Africa for the third time in as many months.

11
World Champion

Nothing can ever take away the pleasure I experienced at winning the world cross-country championship in Lisbon on Sunday 24 March 1985. It was then, and still is, the highlight of my career, because any championship, and especially a world championship, is something to be cherished. Of course it's nice to break a world record, but records are not permanent. At the time you are the fastest person in the world over that distance, but it cannot last. Inevitably the record will be broken, whipped away by somebody else, sometimes by one-hundredth of a second, and you become an also-ran. A world championship, on the other hand, is forever. Unless you are disqualified, nobody can take your medal away and the satisfaction of knowing in your heart that you have taken on and beaten the best athletes on the globe is so intense that it takes days to sink in.

After racing in America I turned up for the cross-country championship in Stellenbosch, where I did a few training sessions with Cornelia Burki, an old friend who, like me, had been born in South Africa but who was now a Swiss national. My preparations went well and on 12 March a set of five 1,000 metres repetitions, with a two-minute rest period between each one, indicated that everything was starting to come together. Times of 2:56, 2:54, 2:51, 2:49 and 2:48 added up to my best 1,000 metres session yet and as I jogged for 16 minutes with Corrie afterwards, I felt I could have done even more.

I knew on my arrival in Portugal that I was in good physical condition, but Ingrid Kristiansen was in the field and she was the favourite. For a change I wasn't under any pressure – I was just another athlete who was in Lisbon to run to the best of her ability – and, although my training had gone well, I didn't see myself as a potential world champion. I would run hard, very hard, and being in a relaxed atmosphere away from the demonstrators and without any political wrangling contributed to my feeling of well-being. I was excited just by being part of such an important event.

The first indication I got that I had the ability to run well came from a surprising source. Pat Butcher, of *The Times*, was not my favourite athletics writer. He had given me a hard time from the moment I arrived in Britain but, at one of my training sessions before the championships, he told me that he thought I might win. It was the first time anybody had told me that I had a chance and it came as a bit of a surprise but, with Ingrid in the field, I didn't allow myself to get too excited at the prospect. In my mind she was going to win and I was just going to give it my best shot.

Although Pat Butcher was the person who first recognized my potential in the race, I was furious with Pieter that he had been invited to the training session in the first place. I felt Butcher had been so unfair to me that I bristled in his presence and I told Pieter afterwards that the press was never to be invited to one of my sessions again.

Another irony in Lisbon was the presence of South African athletic officials at the race. When I had won the South African cross-country championship in 1983 there were many people, myself included, who thought I should have been awarded Springbok colours, but the

101

administrators apparently felt that I was too young. Now their attitude had changed and they were very friendly.

On race day I travelled to the course by bus with the British team. I was in a particularly good frame of mind when we arrived – helped, no doubt by my old ally, lovely warm weather – and I saw Ingrid at the start and we greeted one another. I had got on well with the British team and they sprang to my defence when a South African journalist approached in search of an interview. They told him off in no uncertain terms and I did my strides without any of the hassles I usually encountered in England.

I drew an inside position in the huge field of more than 150, so I knew I had to start fast and, without consciously doing it, found myself in the front after the gun. I couldn't believe it and going round the first bend I thought the pace was too fast. 'Relax,' I told myself. 'Concentrate.' There were mounds, some quite steep, along the route and before the race Pieter had told me to take special care negotiating them because I might lose ground. But nothing could stop me that day and, instead of losing speed on the bumps, I edged further away from Ingrid each time we hit one. After the first lap I heard Pieter and Pat Butcher yelling their encouragement, and because I was feeling so good I decided to increase the pace. I had no trouble over the bumps the second time around and, running downhill towards the finish, I had difficulty comprehending that I still had the lead. Zola Budd was at the head of the field in the world cross-country championships! It was too good to be true. I was running away from the best athletes in the world and they were not going to catch me.

Crossing the line with a 23-seconds lead was the greatest moment of my life. Suddenly everything had been worthwhile; all the training, the trauma of leaving Bloemfontein to become British, the homesickness and the eternal arguments with my coach about the direction in which my career was going. This was the pay-off and I was still coming to grips with my triumph as I put on my tracksuit. On the rostrum I was too shy to raise my arms to acknowledge the applause of the crowd and give vent to the feelings of pure satisfaction that welled within me and Ingrid, who had finished third behind America's Cathy Brantha, lifted up my hand and did it for me. Part of my elation stemmed from beating such a great athlete as Ingrid, and from then on I think we gained a new respect for each other's ability. Poor Ingrid, the medal came off the ribbon as the man doing the presentation was about to put it around her neck, but she didn't seem to mind at all.

My one regret at those championships was missing the men's race because I had to be dope-tested. On a high from my own victory, I was anxious to see who would join me in becoming world champion for 1985, but a delay in answering nature's call put an end to that. That prickle of annoyance was, however, nothing compared to the embarrassment I felt at the behaviour of Jannie and Graham. In the same stand as IAAF president Primo Nebiolo, they forgot where they were and in the excitement of the moment pranced about like a couple of schoolchildren. They were so glad, so triumphant, and they made it obvious that they were South Africans. I was upset by their antics and I wasn't the only one to notice, either. British Amateur Athletic Board promotions director Andy Norman saw what was going on and he gave them hell.

But my embarrassment didn't last long, not with a world championship victory to savour. For the first time in my life I felt I had achieved something really worthwhile. I was so proud of my victory, so glad that some good had finally come out of the trials and tribulations of the previous months that everything became a blur. It took a week to sink in that I had won and all I can remember of the party with the British team that night was that I had a grand time.

12
Hot Streak

My triumph in the world cross-country championship encapsulated the paradox that marked my international career. I was the reluctant runner, the girl who, although unhappy away from her beloved Free State, still relished the challenge of pitting her wits and ability against the best athletes in the world. Running was in my blood and I could never stop but, had I been given the chance to make a decision without any external pressure, I sometimes wonder if I would have utilized my right to claim British citizenship and make the sacrifices necessary to reach the top of women's middle distance running. I don't deny that I wanted the best of both worlds – to train in South Africa where I was comfortable and, at the same time, reap the benefits of pulling on a British vest – but I offer as an extenuating circumstance the fact that, a shy teenager from a rural background, I was easily influenced by those around me.

I don't blame Pieter for pushing me as hard as he did. After all, he had a world class athlete on his hands and he wanted to make the most of it. I appreciate that he made his own sacrifices in an attempt to put me on top of the world, but he was well paid and I question some of his tactics as he attempted to keep my shoulder to the wheel of international competition.

At eighteen I believed almost everything that Pieter said and did most of what he wanted because I wasn't strong enough to resist him. He knew me so well that, even though we had our differences of opinion, I was completely dependent on him. I needed him if I was to run internationally because I was convinced that without him I would have nothing. I could have gone back to my mother, but that's just what he said I would do; and there is no doubt that, had it not been for Pieter, Graham and Jannie, I would not have continued my career after the débâcle of the Olympic Games. Nobody can force you into something as complex as international athletics against your will and – make no mistake – I did want to compete. The world championship proved that conclusively. My problem was being trapped in a web of unfavourable circumstances which made running overseas both appealing and repugnant and Graham, Pieter and Jannie thought they could free me by slowly slotting me into different races in the hope that, once I started running well, I would make my home in England. To do that, though, they reasoned that they had to wean me away from my family, whom they regarded as a bad influence.

After the world championships I had a short break in Bloemfontein, and then it was back to Stellenbosch to prepare for the track season. I was still the reluctant athlete and when Ma dropped me at the Bloemfontein airport I was crying. Pieter and Jannie picked me up in Cape Town for the drive to Stellenbosch and, although it is a beautiful part of the world, I hated it. All I had to occupy me was my running and after a particularly bad day and midway through a sleepless night, I decided that enough was enough, so I packed my bags, jumped into my car and set off on the 1,000 kilometres drive to Bloemfontein.

I had never driven so far alone before and I was frightened. After all, it was 3 o'clock in the morning, but I was determined to get to Bloemfontein. Following the signs on an unfamiliar road, I played the devil's advocate in my

105

mind: 'You still have time to turn around, and nobody will know what happened.' 'No, press on. You must keep going.' In the tradition of an athlete who never pulls out of a race before the finish, I kept driving and after just ten hours on the road I was home. Ma got the shock of her life when I turned up at the front door and I'm afraid I gave Jannie and Pieter a terrible scare. They didn't have a clue where I was and I'm sure it crossed their minds that I had committed suicide. I heard later that they looked for me everywhere; and it took me three weeks to go back to Stellenbosch to sort out the whole sorry mess. They all spent time with me and in the end Pieter used the old argument that I would be a nobody unless I achieved something overseas. But he let something slip when he told me he 'didn't want to coach normal schoolchildren'. In other words, he was interested only in training a world class athlete and the prestige that would come with it. Pieter did OK financially, too. My father had given him a cut of the *Mail* money; I paid him and all his expenses overseas were covered either by the trust or by sponsors.

I resumed training for the 1985 track season and moved into a town house that had a small garden. A friend, Miensie Roux, came to stay with me, which was nice as I was desperate for company, and Fraaier made the trip from Bloemfontein to Stellenbosch. Things were looking up and, under Pieter's watchful eye, I trained well in April and May, reaching a career best of 160 kilometres a week.

When it came to my nineteenth birthday I let Miensie into a little secret. I have always loved cakes and ever since I could remember I had wanted one in the shape of a train for my birthday. My dream came true when Miensie ordered a train cake from a bakery. When she collected it the man behind the counter asked, 'How old is the little boy?' 'Four', said Miensie, who left the shop in hysterics. I spent my days training and doing some studying through Unisa; but although Miensie and her pole-vaulter boyfriend Louis van Zyl were good company, I yearned for something more.

106

I didn't have long to wait because it was off to Britain in June. After an indifferent start to my season, when I clocked a dreadful 9:01 over 3,000 metres in Belfast, things started looking up when I finished first in 8:44.54 against France and the Soviet Union at Gateshead. I was quite pleased with that performance, but my rematch against Mary Decker-Slaney over 3,000 metres in the Peugeot–Talbot Games on 20 July was a disaster.

Arranged by Graham and promoter Andy Norman, it was a re-run of the Continental Homes race all over again – hyped up by the media and blown out of all proportion. It was regarded as a 'happening' and the publicity blast detracted from any athletic merit the race might have had. On top of that, the 'For Sale' sign was back around my neck. Give Graham his due: as a businessman he got me a sensational deal – £90,000 was a huge amount of money – but, with the arrangement public knowledge, I was perceived as a money-grabber. There was a lot of negative feedback about my so-called mercenary attitude and what really hurt was the fact that at the time the deal was struck I was not aware of how much money was involved. It took the shine off the race and I told Pieter weeks beforehand that I didn't want to get involved. 'It's too late,' my trustees told me. 'Everything has been arranged. Why not take the opportunity to make some money, because if you don't somebody else will.'

Things might have been different if the rematch had been 'just another race' in which Mary happened to be one of the competitors; then I could simply have turned up and run. But the money and circumstances surrounding the 'grudge match' made it impossible for me to treat it seriously. This seemed to me to be a prime example of commercial exploitation. Apart from me, a lot of people were going to benefit financially and because it was so artificial I didn't see how it would prove anything. My relationship with Pieter became strained again and my training erratic as I battled to achieve the mental strength

I required for the equivalent of a boxing prize-fight. A good session would be followed by a bad one and Pieter was at his wits' end.

'Listen to me,' he said, 'either you start training properly or I won't coach you any more.' That put me between a rock and a hard place because I would do anything Pieter asked and I battled on grimly. But my heart wasn't in it and I was very lacking in motivation on race day.

Mary and I had little to say to each other at the track apart from 'Hi', and there was none of the antagonism that the press had been so desperately hoping for. It was our first meeting since the fall and Mary looked so relaxed, while I just wanted to get it over with. That wasn't the right attitude at all and, worst of all, I didn't care. I was fit enough to give a good account of myself but after the gun I ran mechanically. 'One lap gone, two laps gone, three laps gone.' It was like the Olympic final after the fall. 'Finish this farce and get out of here', I thought and, instead of making a race of it, I lost interest, running slower and slower. I finished fourth in 8:45.43 to Mary's 8:32.91 and walked off the track a very disillusioned young lady.

At home in Guildford that night, Pieter came into my room and was really nice. I had been expecting the worst after my dismal performance but his attitude was 'Don't worry about it.' That was a pleasant change, but Pieter was a different man the next day. 'What was wrong with you?' he demanded. 'If you had held on you would have run your best time. Now Les Jones and Andy Norman are upset.' Later, at a braai at the hotel where Graham was staying with his wife Trish, Pieter warned me that unless I changed my attitude and started producing the performances he knew I was capable of, I would not be able to pick my races any more.

Race selection depends on your status: top runners receive invitations to the best events and they can even dictate to a certain extent against whom they want to run: 'No, I don't want that athlete in the field . . . yes, she's all right.' I felt it was almost as if Pieter was playing me off against other athletes and I was sad that our relationship had sunk to this level, because Pieter had been such a tower of strength in the past. I was aware of the fact that Pieter and Carin were unhappy in England and would have liked nothing better than to return to South Africa, and it made me feel guilty. But I also felt that Pieter's attitude had changed from one of concern about me as a person to one of worry about his reputation. Whereas I had in the past run for enjoyment and personal fulfilment, I was now running for money and prestige.

Not even a victory three days after the Decker charade could buoy up Pieter's spirits. Perhaps he was still annoyed over my poor showing against Mary, but I expected something more than a drawn face when I won a mile race in Edinburgh. This time all I had to cope with was demonstrators, who put up anti-apartheid banners in the hope that they would gain some TV exposure. It didn't work, though, because ITV refused to televise the race unless the banners were removed. The banners stayed up and the ITV cameras were removed – and I admire them for sticking to their guns. Without publicity, the demonstrators were powerless and not even a skinhead who ran on to the track during the second lap could disrupt the race. We just ran around him as he clutched with white fingers to the lip on the inside of the track, and I had little trouble winning in a pleasing 4:22.14, with splits of 65 seconds, 2:11 and 3:16.

'Aren't you glad I ran well?' I asked Pieter. 'Yes, I'm glad', he replied. Well, he could have fooled me. At the very least he could have exhibited some show of elation and I began wondering just what I had to do to please him. This wasn't how an athlete/coach affiliation was supposed to work and I believed that, instead of me having to soothe him all the time, he should be encouraging me.

Needing a good race to bolster my confidence, I turned

my attention to the Women's AAA championship in Birmingham on 27 July. I would have preferred running in a race in Oslo on the same day, but was advised that it would be good politics to compete in my 'home' championship. There weren't too many 'name' athletes on the Birmingham programme and the British board made it known that I would be doing myself a favour by supporting them instead of running abroad. I obliged by winning the 3,000 metres in 8:50.5 – quite a good time, but that didn't seem to impress my coach.

The Birmingham race indicated that I was approaching peak form, and Pieter let me off the leash for a few days so that I could train with Corrie in Switzerland. Suddenly, everything started falling into place as I put in some really good sessions with my old friend. Something clicked in those four days, and when I returned to England I was on the verge of the most successful twenty-nine days in my track career.

A 20-minute run on 8 August with Pieter was the prelude to a mile race at Gateshead which I won in 4:22.96 – a personal best. That was more like it, particularly as my 1,500 metres split was 4:03, compared to the world junior record of 4:01.81 I had set in Port Elizabeth the previous year.

My next step was Moscow and it was a real treat to travel behind the Iron Curtain. Being on a South African passport, Pieter had to stay behind and he never let me forget that I ran what I regard as my best track race without him. It was the 3,000 metres in the Europa Cup on 17 August and I went to the front from the gun and stayed there, winning with a sprint from the Soviet Union's Zamira Zaitseva and Ulrike Bruns, of East Germany, in a British record of 8:35.32. I covered the first 1,000 metres in 2:50, the next in 2:55 and the last 1,000 metres in 2:55 – a good, hard piece of running which left me drained but very happy. You always feel good after a personal best performance and I went to bed that night knowing that I had done something worthwhile.

110

Zurich was the venue for my third personal best in a row when, on 21 August, I ran the mile in the Weltklasse meeting against my old foe, Mary Decker. I couldn't beat her or edge out Maricica Puica for second place, but there was nothing wrong with coming in 4:17.57 to Mary's world record 4:16.71. My time was a Commonwealth record and I had edged closer to the four-minute barrier with a 1,500 metres split of 4:00.79, another personal best.

Five days later I was in London for a 5,000 metres showdown against Ingrid Kristiansen; and Pieter, Carin, Ma, Graham and I piled into the car for the trip to Crystal Palace. After a string of fine performances I was nice and relaxed and Ingrid and I agreed to take turns in setting the pace. The only trouble that day came from sponsors McVitie's biscuits, who were furious that their name had been cut off my race number. With me running a world record, they lost a lot of media mileage, but fortunately I wasn't to blame. The organizers did the damage when, unable to find a No. 9 for me, they got hold of a six, cut the name off and gave it to me to pin on upside-down!

That 5,000 metres was an eye-opener for anyone who thought that breaking a world record required something really special – a supreme effort, the ability to surpass the threshold of pain, the will to run into the unknown. It sounds blasé but, maybe because the 5,000 metres was a relatively new event and we were only starting to push the barriers back, the race at Crystal Palace on 26 August was one of my easiest. Granted, I was in the middle of what was, for me, a hot streak, with a personal best time almost every time I stepped on to the track during that magical twenty-nine days, but that 5,000 metres was reminiscent of the cross-country in Lisbon in that I had the ability to 'flow'. I was comfortable throughout, feeling no strain when Ingrid set the pace, and I was thrilled with my time of 14:48.07.

Brussels on 30 August for the Van Damme meeting and another appointment with Mary was a different matter

111

entirely. A hard and fast 1,500 metres race was won by Mary in 3:57.27, and I was third in 3:59.96, the first time I had beaten four minutes. There had been talk of withdrawing me from the Brussels race, but I only discovered later that it had revolved around money. Graham had wanted me to receive the same appearance fee as Mary, which I didn't think was realistic under the circumstances. Mary was on a high at that time and I the pretender to her crown and, anyway, money was not that important to me. I had Jannie and Graham looking after my interests and I trusted them to do the best they could, but in my view that didn't extend to putting the squeeze on meeting organizers. Being paid just to line up and race for big prizes puts the pressure on and, for me at least, inhibits performance. I prefer to earn my living from endorsements obtained as a result of good performances, and I was annoyed that Graham could even think of using financial considerations as leverage in arranging my races or, worse, threaten to withdraw me if his demands were not met.

By the time I got to the Grand Prix finals in Rome on 9 September I was so tired from all the racing that I told Pieter I wished it was all over. The Olympics and the rematch forgotten, I was again up against Mary and Puica but, as in my previous clash against Mary, the past was forgotten. This was real athletics, every woman for herself, without promoters baying in the background, and my attitude and the atmosphere were totally different. I was good, but not quite classy enough for the Olympic champion and the girl all America thought deserved the gold. I kept contact with Mary for seven laps of the seven-and-a-half laps, but was outsprinted in the straight and beaten into third place. Mary recorded my 'dream' time of 8:25.83 – how I wanted to break 8:26! – and I clocked 8:29.83 for my third Commonwealth record in a season which must have given Pieter a lot of hope.

The Grand Prix in Rome, when my 2,000 metres split was 5:39.2, was my final track race of 1985 and I returned to Stellenbosch to write exams and have a short break before getting ready for the defence of my cross-country title in Neuchâtel, Switzerland. I obviously overdid it – in some weeks my seven-day total was 160 kilometres – and I ended up hurting my right hamstring again during a track session. It was the beginning of the end as far as sparkling performances were concerned. Apart from the 1986 world cross-country championship in March 1986, a world indoor 3,000 metres record in February of the same year and winning the British AAA 1,500 metres, I didn't have much to look forward to and the injury reignited the tension between Pieter and me. 'Meneer' (I always called him that, it's the Afrikaans equivalent of 'Sir' in English schools), 'my leg is hurting.' Back came the predictable reply: 'Zola, it's all in your head.'

A difficult man to please, first places in two 10 kilometres road races in America (Rosemont on 24 November and San Diego on 1 December), were not enough to console Pieter. For many, winning is everything, but victory in slow times – 32:29 in Rosemont and 33:15 in San Diego – was not good enough and I had the feeling that I had let Pieter down. But my leg was hurting and I adopted the fatalistic attitude that I would run until I couldn't move another step. Then, maybe, I would be believed.

113

13
'Take That'

The year 1986 started as one of great expectations with the defence of my world cross-country championship, the Commonwealth Games and the European championships. It was also the year that Pieter started teaching at the Paul Roos Gymnasium in Stellenbosch and he was not very happy about it. The morning he had to go to the school for his first day of work I saw him standing next to the car and kicking the wheels in frustration. I could understand how he felt because his appointment, 'arranged' by Jannie, had antagonized a number of people in Stellenbosch.

It was also a difficult time for me in that I was travelling to England for the first time without Pieter and it seemed like a step into the unknown. Pieter had played such a key role in my life, especially after I walked out on my father, and I was sure I would be lost without him. Sure, we had our disagreements, but I depended on Pieter more than anyone else as far as my athletics was concerned and we were still a team. Pieter and Zola – two complex people thrown together in a relationship in which each needed the other. It was almost love and hate, but I felt I couldn't function effectively without him and I believed and did most of what he told me. The day before I was to leave for England I visited him at the school and he wished me well and gave

114

me a letter, which I kept in the back of my Bible and read often. A message of encouragement, the letter was like a prescription for motivation in which Pieter, noting that I would be on my own, urged me to do my best.

There was another letter waiting for me in Guildford. It was from Marea Hartman, the honorary secretary of the Women's Amateur Athletic Association, who was clearly anxious about the amount of time I was spending in South Africa. Dated 17 January 1986, it read:

Dear Zola,

Commonwealth Games – Eligibility of competitors

As I think you know, I hope you are interested in being considered as a member of the English Women's Commonwealth Games Team at Edinburgh this summer. Because of this it is important now to draw your attention to the eligibility rule of the Commonwealth Games Federation. This sets out the conditions for representing a country at the Commonwealth Games. A copy of the Commonwealth Games Federation's rule book is enclosed and the eligibility rule is Article 34 on page 22.

Article 34.1 requires a competitor to be a citizen of a Commonwealth country and you of course satisfy this requirement with your British passport.

Article 34.2 does not apply in your case.

However, Article 34.3 is important in your case and it is worth my setting it out below in full:–

'If an eligible competitor wishes to represent a Commonwealth country other than that of his birth, he must have resided therein for a minimum period of 6 months during the 12 months prior to the closing date of the individual entries for the Commonwealth Games concerned or his domicile, "permanent home", or normal place of residence must be in that Commonwealth Country.'

For you to be eligible to be a member of the English Team in Edinburgh, you will either have had to have resided in England for a minimum of six months during the twelve months prior to the closing date for entries for Edinburgh (i.e. 6th July 1986), or your domicile, permanent home, or normal place of residence must be in England.

Would you therefore please let me know:

(a) whether your plans are such that you will have resided in England for at least six months during the twelve month period ending 6th July 1986; or

(b) whether you would satisfy the alternative requirement that your domicile, 'permanent home' or normal place of residence is in England.

I am sure you will understand the publicity that your prospective membership of the England Team at Edinburgh may attract. By satisfying the six month residence in England test you would, I feel, put the matter beyond doubt. The residence in England does not of course have to be continuous and can be spread over the twelve months prior to 6th July 1986.

Please do not hesitate to contact me should you have any queries on this.

Assuming that everything was going to be fine, this was my reply:

Dear Miss Hartman

Thank you for your letter of January 17th 1986 about the Commonwealth Games.

I see no difficulty in meeting the residence requirements as outlined in your letter.

I am looking forward to taking part in the

Commonwealth Games in Edinburgh during July.
Kindest regards
Zola Budd

At that stage, it didn't seem as though there would be any difficulty over my qualification to run in the Commonwealth Games, but I had no idea then of the lengths to which the Commonwealth Games Federation would go in an attempt to force me out of the Games at Edinburgh. The knives were to come out later when the amount of time I spent in South Africa came under the microscope and, although my legal opinion suggested that I could successfully challenge the Federation in court, I eventually withdrew, beaten down by the immense pressure and disillusioned by a leg injury I knew would prevent me from running well anyway.

I touched down in England on Thursday 23 January and was scheduled to race the next day in the British indoor championships at Cosford in Birmingham. Mel Batty, of Brooks shoes, picked me up at the airport and took me to Guildford, but when I saw him the next day I was so depressed and lonely without Pieter that I told him I didn't want to run. I also phoned Graham to tell him how much I missed Pieter and longed for his company in England, but the only advice he could give me was: 'Don't worry, everything will pass.' If Graham had been in the same room as me I would have thrown something at him. Didn't he understand that I was still vulnerable and needed a strong hand to guide me? Jannie rang me later and I slammed the phone down in a fit of pique. Here I was, in a cold, miserable climate while Pieter was sitting in Stellenbosch where it was lovely and warm.

Mel was caught in the middle and, after he contacted Jannie, told me that I didn't have to run if I didn't want to. The lure was a suggestion that I accompany him to Cosford anyway, 'just to have a look', and I took the bait. On the way

117

we stopped at a really tacky motorway café and, being a sucker for food of any kind, I ate to my heart's content – yoghurt, fish and chips, bread and cake. I was ravenous and when at last I wiped my mouth with the napkin I wondered how I could possibly race that afternoon on a full stomach.

Luckily for me the race was postponed – there had been a power failure at the stadium – and I was very relieved. We stayed at the Holiday Inn and I went for a jog with Yvonne Murray and a couple of other girls. The next day I ran my best indoor 1,500 metres in 4:06.07, in spite of approaching the race in great trepidation.

That gave my confidence a big boost and Pieter's absence was made up for in some measure when my steeplechaser friend D.B. Prinsloo flew in from South Africa to stay with me for a couple of weeks. It was all part of the plan to help me settle down and I was so glad to see him. That my friends were prepared to travel overseas to train with me and give me companionship was a great comfort to me and D.B. was wonderful. While many male athletes like to 'show up' top women competitors in training, racing away to assert their superiority, D.B. was the perfect training partner. As we warmed up for our first session together by running 5 kilometres at a kilometre pace of 3:50 on a bitterly cold day, I asked him what the 'white stuff' was on his face. The poor man from sunny South Africa, he was running in sleet and snow and his moustache had frozen! But he stuck it out and, wearing rain suits, we went on to run 1,200-metre repetitions, followed by a 5 kilometres 'warm-down'.

My training went well with my South African friend, who, incidentally, was courting Elizna van Zyl, and my next race was a cross-country in Peterborough. Again it was freezing. I travelled to Peterborough with D.B. and Mel Batty and met Andy Norman and Fatima Whitbread at the race. It was so cold that Andy refused to leave the sanctuary of the car – a few minutes in the open and you were chilled to the bone – but again I had a good race, winning the 5.7 kilometres event in a pleasing 18:09. After-wards I went with Andy to the prize-giving and he echoed Marea Hartman's warning that if I didn't spend more time in England there would be problems for me if I wanted to run in the Edinburgh Commonwealth Games. Repeated visits to South Africa, he said, would not be tolerated by the authorities and, although I understood my predicament, I wasn't sure how to handle the situation. The more I thought about living and training in a climate I disliked, the more I rebelled against cutting my family and friends out of my life for an extended period. I was young, I missed my family, warm weather was essential if I was to train to the best of my ability and I recoiled at the prospect of going through the track season without Pieter.

In Guildford after the cross-country I became quite depressed. How could I cope on my own, I wondered. In what had become a familiar pattern for me in times of stress, my training suffered, and that was after only two weeks in England. Doing mile repetitions with D.B. around Stoke Park one day, I just gave up. 'It's hopeless,' I told him, 'I can't concentrate.' It felt as though I couldn't breathe without Pieter, let alone force myself out into the cold every morning. I needed Pieter's understanding and advice and when I rang him he did his best to cheer me up.

It's odd how sometimes an athlete performs beyond expectations when training has not been as intense as it should have been and this point was brought home on 8 February in the indoor match between Britain and Hungary, where I was to run the 3,000 metres. I had slacked off, relying on a 90-minute run five days before the race, six easy miles in interval training on 5 February and easy jogs, but that turned out to be all I needed! Still feeling sorry for myself, I was on the phone to Pieter just before the match with the same old story – 'I've had enough, I don't want to run.' But Pieter was getting tired of my complaining: 'Buck up your ideas,' he said. 'Show them what you're made of.'

Feeling very low, I pulled myself together and took Pieter's advice, aided by the presence of *The Times* athletics correspondent Pat Butcher, whom I saw with the press contingent at Cosford, and British shot-put star Judy Oakes. Both were members of the 'anti-Budd' brigade and both had been critical of my selection for Britain. Butcher, in particular, had been very harsh about me in *The Times* and the sight when I got to the track of him with the press and Judy, who was throwing, made me feel incredibly aggressive. 'I'll show them all right', I thought as I faced the starter and I set off at a murderous pace. The first 400 metres was much too fast, but I settled down, concentrated and really turned it on every time I came down the straight.

It was as if all the frustration of the last few months was being released in what was, for me, a surprising show of power. With each step I seemed to make up for all the political wrangling, the constant criticism that I wasn't 'British' enough, all the hateful things that they were writing about me in the press. When I won the race in a world record of 8:39.79 I looked at the pressmen and with great inner satisfaction said to them mentally, 'Take that. I've got you this time. Now you will have to write something positive about me.'

The mellow glow of knowing that I had run well filtered through my body and I was proud of myself and really confident for the first time in weeks. Not that I showed it, even when Yvonne Murray asked me afterwards how it felt. Running was still a very private thing for me and I found it difficult expressing my delight and satisfaction to anybody, even my family. My mother, for example, never asks me how I feel about running in general or even specific moments of triumph, such as the first world cross-country title. I hide everything inside and examine it when I lie in bed and thank God for giving me the ability to run well. My diary entry for 8 February 1986 said simply: '15h20 women's 3,000m Cosford Brit. v Hungary. 1 8:39.79 (best time) (wr)' and it was the same after my victory in Lisbon: '14h40

An ecstatic Graham Boonzaier (right) and Jannie Momberg celebrate my victory in the 1985 cross-country championships in Lisbon.

The clock tells it all, or most of it, after my victory over Ingrid Kristiansen in London on 16 August 1985. I was officially timed at 14.48.07, the second time I had set a world record over 5,000 metres.

With my friend and occasional training partner Cornelia Burki in 1986, when I spent time with her in Switzerland.

In the pack before I made my move in the first kilometre of the 1986 world cross-country championships in Neuchatel, Switzerland in 1986.

I wonder what the future holds as I face the media in January 1987 at a Press conference called to announce that I am back in training with a new coach, Harry Wilson (right). Harry looks equally pensive, while on the left is British Amateur Athletic Board official Tony Ward.

Out on my own in the successful defence of my world cross-country title in Neuchatel in 1986. I was worried that I had made a mistake by running barefoot, but I was able to cope with the slippery conditions.

One of my last races in England, the world cross-country trials at Gateshead on 30 January 1988. I finished fourth behind Angela Tooby and would run two more cross-countries before returning to South Africa.

Cuddling my dog, Fraaier, at home in Bloemfontein in 1988.

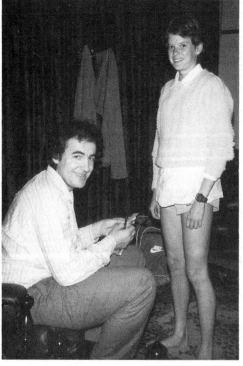

The man who saved my career, applied kinesiologist Ron Holder, during a testing session. The Doctor, as I call him, pinpointed muscular imbalances in my body and corrected them with wedges in my shoes and extensive exercise routines.

On a training run in South Africa in 1988 when wedges, or orthotics, inserted in my shoes by Dr Ron Holder helped me get over a crippling leg injury.

At home with Ma and my sister Estelle.

I'm not much of a cook but here I give it a try, watched by the family maid, Maria, and her daughter, Mampho.

Mike and I catch everybody by surprise by announcing our engagement in August 1988. Sharing our joy are my dog, Basjan, and cat, Sangiro.

My brother Quintus was behind the camera when we signed the register. Ma is behind me with my father-in-law Mike Pieterse and his wife, Bettie.

Mike and I on our big day, with flower girls Lucian van der Westhuizen and Jenny Budd.

World Cross-Country championship Lisbon. 1. Z Budd 15:01.' I have never gloated about my success or sought praise because I get my kicks from knowing in my heart I have achieved something worthwhile.

I didn't compete in the national cross-country championship in 1986 because the British officials could not guarantee my safety after the débâcle the previous year, when I was forced off the track, and I was pre-selected to defend my title in Neuchâtel in Switzerland. That meant I could slip back to South Africa for a brief visit in February and it was like a tonic for me to see my family again and spend time with Pieter, talking and training. That was a treat but so too was buying my house in Guildford.

I got the keys before my flying visit to Stellenbosch and was like a child with a new toy. It was so exciting buying everything I needed and D.B. and I combed the shops of Guildford in search of furniture, cutlery, crockery and all the other comforts of home. D.B. was a star, washing the floors for me and lugging my purchases all the way to Eastgate Gardens. They say that women love shopping, and generally I am no exception, but I must admit that even I got tired. But it was still a lot of fun. I went to one shop so many times that the assistants got to know me well, but I always had an eye open for a bargain and they had lots of things on 'special offer'. I was, however, still sensitive and I was too embarrassed to go back after the day the man behind the counter told me that the shop would soon have the salt and pepper sets on special if I carried on with my spending spree.

With the cross-country championships approaching, Pieter got leave from the school in Stellenbosch to be with me for such an important occasion, but Carin arrived in Guildford ahead of him and was confronted by a half-empty house. My furniture had not yet arrived and we had to sleep on the carpet, watching my new television set and eating chocolate peanuts. At least I had some beds by the time

121

Pieter arrived, and I was feeling on top of the world when we left for Switzerland.

My sweet tooth still very much in evidence, I took a huge bag of 'dolly mixture' confectionery to Switzerland and wolfed it down when the rest of the English girls were watching their diet. While they selected fruit and carefully took the skin off the chicken, I ate sweets, lucky to be one of those people who don't have to count calories or worry about health fads.

The day before the race I went with the team to look at the course, and I had a feeling I might do well as the weather was glorious, sunny and warm. What a contrast the next morning when, peering out of the window, I saw sleet! That was the last thing I wanted and the prospect of running in cold, muddy conditions added to my nervousness. A friend gave me a book by Paul Galico called *Jennie* and I tried to read it in the tent at the race venue. Even now, when I see that book my stomach turns, as I am reminded how apprehensive I was before my second world cross-country championship. I was so tense I felt ill and conditions underfoot when I warmed up increased my anxiety. It was so slippery and muddy that I had difficulty doing strides and I tried wearing racing flats – with no success. That left spikes, but I had a communication gap with them; wondering what to wear, I saw Mel Batty in the warm-up area. He walked around with me and left when an agitated Pieter arrived. My coach thought Mel had been trying to talk me into wearing spikes – after all, Mel worked for shoe company Brooks with whom I had a contract – and suggested that I run barefoot. A short while later, though, when he saw people slipping and sliding, Pieter said spikes would be best, but by that time I had packed my shoes away and was squelching around in cold mud. It was dreadful and my feet were frozen, but I didn't have time to put on spikes.

I immediately took the lead from the gun and, aware of the treacherous surface, knew at 400 metres that I could be in trouble. Barefoot on firm ground is one thing, running without shoes in mud quite another. 'Oh no, there's going to be problems today,' I thought after 400 metres and, in an attempt to give myself a cushion, I ran hard to open up a gap in the first kilometre. Going barefoot had been a big mistake as I struggled to keep my footing on the slippery downhills and the pack was closing in. To make up for the ground I lost downhill, I accelerated on level ground; and, looking back, I realize just how fit I was on that day. At a severe disadvantage, I could still assert my authority and I was in a way playing with the rest of the field. It's a wonderful feeling to be in peak condition, to know that your body will respond every time you ask it for one more effort, and nobody was going to deprive me of my second world title; American Lynn Jennings was second. While naturally very pleased with myself, I didn't experience the elation of Lisbon the previous year, rather a sense of relief. I had been so nervous going into the race, and afterwards it was a case of 'Phew, thank goodness I came through that unscathed.'

Another hamstring injury just after my birthday in May took the shine off a year that had promised so much. It happened when I was doing circuit training in Guildford with Minke van der Walt, who had joined me as a member of the 'Budd shift' – friends who were prepared to give up their time to brave the English climate and give me moral support. The hamstring pull was a lot more serious than people, including Pieter, realized and coupled with the drama surrounding my participation in the Commonwealth Games, was the turning-point in my career. I still had a few good performances left in me, but the injury was to remain a nagging pain, a throbbing reminder that all was not well in the Budd camp, physically, emotionally or politically.

The fact that Pieter, Jannie and Graham all initially failed to realize the seriousness of the injury really irked me and it was the sore hamstring as much as anything else that finally prompted me to withdraw from the Commonwealth Games

123

in Edinburgh in July. Bewildered by the controversy my trips to South Africa had stirred up, hurt by the antagonism of the African countries, indignant at the attitude of the Commonwealth Games Federation, at a low ebb emotionally from my clashes with Pieter and literally hamstrung, I reached the point where I was simply fed up with the whole thing.

Especially galling was the fact that I am certain I would have 'won' had I pursued my right to participate in the Games to the bitter end. I spent hours with lawyers – and £13,000 – seeking legal opinion on my eligibility after the Federation decided on 13 July that I was ineligible; their expert advice was that I could mount a successful court action. But was it worth it? Not in the state I was in.

The pressure over that period was enormous and with the press camped on my doorstep from dawn to midnight life seemed intolerable. I escaped one day by going to a friend's house and from there to the station, where I took a train to London; I spent the whole day in Hyde Park enjoying the solitude. On another occasion while the Commonwealth Games 'war' was raging, I went to Port Isaac in Cornwall with Pieter. Anything to get away, although I detected a shift in Pieter's attitude as we relaxed in the West Country. Sitting outside one evening, Pieter asked me what I wanted to achieve in the European championships in Stuttgart and my reply was 'A medal'. 'No,' said Pieter, 'your motivation is all wrong. You mustn't be content with a medal, you must go for gold.' We had never differed on things like this before and I found it disturbing and a portent of things to come, when Pieter would expect nothing but the best while I was physically unable to produce the goods.

Very aware of my injury, I won the Women's AAA 1,500 metres in Birmingham in 4:01.93 and on 30 June went to Belfast to compete over 3,000 metres in the Ulster Games. A wet, slippery track meant I had to wear spikes for that race and I could feel the hamstring protesting. Expecting it to pull at any moment, I got home safely in 8:34.43 and started taking anti-inflammatory tablets shortly afterwards as the pain became more severe. Next up was the 2,000 metres in the Peugeot-Talbot Games at Crystal Palace on 11 July and by now I was really suffering. Pieter was in England for the main part of the track season, but I felt I did not get the sympathy or help I wanted from him and not even third place was good enough for him. Puica won the race in 5:28.69, Yvonne Murray was second and I crossed the line in 5:30.19. My leg was so painful I could hardly walk, but more important to my coach was what he perceived as a lack of motivation on my part.

Five days later we were in Barcelona, and I came fourth in an 800 metres race in 2:07. For an athlete of my class, a time of 2:07 was shocking. It must have been apparent that I had a problem other than a lack of motivation, but Pieter shook me to the core when, the following day, he remarked that I should continue my international career without him. We were sitting outside a Spanish café, Pieter drinking coffee and I tea, when he dropped his bombshell: 'You haven't raced well since I have been in England,' he told me. 'There's no use me staying on and it would be better if you continued on your own. I don't think I should be involved any more.'

I was appalled. Was this my coach talking, the man with whom I had been through so much, the man I relied on? I was stunned that he was prepared to call it quits over a cup of coffee in Spain. 'But what am I going to do?' I asked, feeling as though it was me, not Mary, who had fallen in an Olympic final. 'Well,' came the reply, 'you can always go to Switzerland to stay with Corrie Burki.'

On the aircraft back to England I was still in a state of shock. Ironically, I was seated next to a triple jumper named Francis Dodo who was, I think, from Ghana. He was also upset – and for a reason with which I could identify. A number of countries, among them Ghana, had decided to boycott the Edinburgh Commonwealth Games because of the rebel rugby tour to South Africa and, like me, he wanted to take part. So we both sat in the plane, pictures of dejection, each wrestling with a private tragedy.

Pieter, however, had another card to play in a game which was rapidly deteriorating into a farce. He had reshuffled the pack overnight and when we arrived in England he told me not to worry. 'Everything is fine,' he said. 'We'll work things out.' He had gone from one extreme to the other and I was baffled by his attitude. I didn't know where I stood with him and it would be some months before the final break – months in which I was constantly confused about the nature of our relationship.

My leg held out for a trip to Zurich for the Weltklasse meeting on 13 August when I finished third in the 3,000 metres behind Ingrid Kristiansen and, on my return, Graham collected me at the airport and I stayed with him at Harpenden. I was to race next at Hendon over 1,500 metres on 17 August and I was scared to death when I rang Pieter in Stellenbosch to tell him that Kirsty Wade and Shirley Bailey were in the field.

'Oh, I don't know if you should run,' said Pieter. 'You are not that good.' A non-committal coach was the last thing I needed and when I asked him what tactics I should use, he replied: 'I don't know . . . wait and see what they do.'

Wait and see! I knew I could beat them but, with a sore leg, I needed help and advice. I didn't get it from Pieter but I did get a confidence boost from Frank Henderson, who was to become Liz Lynch's coach. I met him on the morning of the race and felt a lot better when he told me that I could run well. 'You can still run fast,' he said. 'Run tactically and you can win.'

That helped, but I was still in a state warming up. I did my usual strides, wondering if my leg would hold out, and then did another, and another, just to see if I would cope. I attacked from the start, going for broke and when Kirsty came past me with 300 metres to run I thought it was all over. I wasn't going down without a fight, though, and was astonished to discover that I stayed in contact when I accelerated. I accelerated some more and won the race in 4:05.56, which, I felt, was pretty good considering the bad leg.

Now, only the European championships were left and I was hardly in shape to double in the 1,500 and 3,000 metres as I had originally planned. I had to take anti-inflammatory tablets all the time and nobody realized, or wanted to realize, that I was hurting. This was no ordinary hamstring strain and I became dependent on the tablets. They were my saviours and when I was staying with Graham in Harpenden prior to leaving for Stuttgart and the tablets ran out, I drove to Guildford and back just to fetch some more. The tablets relieved the pain, but as soon as I did a few hard training sessions it came back.

It was at this stage that I started thinking seriously about spending less time in South Africa. The Barcelona incident with Pieter had worried me and the Hendon race had proved that I was becoming more independent of my coach. I was, anyway, getting tired of flying back and forth and I liked the idea of enrolling at the University of Surrey. I told Les Jones and Graham how I felt and even Pieter, who seemed to accept it. I wanted to be based more permanently in one place because I was missing out on so much. You don't have a lifestyle worth talking about when you are on an aircraft all the time. There are no basics, no routine like being able to read before going to bed or doing something specific at weekends. My life lacked stability and security and being a British citizen, it was natural for me to consider putting roots down in England. I went to the University of Surrey, got hold of all the information and brochures I could lay my hands on and took the lot to Stuttgart where, coincidentally, we stayed on a university campus. There I was able to wander around and imagine what it would be like as a student. I visited the library and had a tremendous urge to lose myself among all the books, to study, to become part of an institution where I

127

could achieve something tangible. Until now, I only had my athletics and with an unsympathetic coach and a throbbing leg injury, that part of my life was cracking, about to tumble down.

But first, before I could do any serious planning, I had some races to run and going to the track for the 3,000 metres final, I was quite nervous. Although I had received treatment from the British team physiotherapist, I was all too aware that my leg could give way at any moment and, to make matters worse, the track was wet, which meant I had to wear spikes. There was only one thing to do and that was run hard from the gun and pray that I could hold on. Suddenly aggression replaced the nervousness and I ran hard for five laps and was only caught on the last lap, when Olga Bondarenko and Puica overtook me. 'Oh well,' I thought, 'third would be good.' I thought I was good for a medal until I hit the straight and heard footsteps behind me. It was Yvonne Murray and, unable to sustain the pressure, my legs gave way with 80 metres to run and I finished fourth. Taking the injury into account, I was pleased with my performance, although I doubted the wisdom of doubling in the 1,500 metres.

I told Pieter I would withdraw from the 1,500 metres but, with nothing to lose, changed my mind. He may have been worried about my injury but he didn't show it and even Corrie misunderstood me. 'My leg is sore,' I said. 'It's hurting.' 'Don't worry,' was her reply. 'Everybody is hurting.'

Pieter's tactical advice before the 1,500 metres was to make a break for it after 800 metres which, in retrospect, was silly. But I did it all the same, was hauled back with 200 metres to go and finished a dismal ninth. I wasn't surprised because I knew I was too slow to stand a real chance and I was far from fit. I ran the 1,500 metres from memory and chalked it up to experience.

My track season finished, I returned to Guildford and took up cycling just to keep myself occupied. Jannie told me he would organize the best possible specialists to examine my leg but it was far too late. I had needed expert medical opinion ten weeks previously, not after the European championships. Pieter kept his thoughts pretty much to himself and on the flight back to South Africa was strangely quiet. Eventually, he could contain himself no longer and when I asked him what was bothering him he wanted to know how he was going to explain my poor performances to people in South Africa. 'What am I going to tell them?' he asked. 'You've run so badly this year and I'm the one who is going to get the blame.' We were close to breaking-point now. Our approach to running was oceans apart and I couldn't understand why he was so worried about the newspapers. Tell them I was injured, I thought, it's that simple.

In Bloemfontein, where I was only supposed to stay for two weeks, I went to see a specialist who told me my right hamstring was too short. I did corrective exercises and had physiotherapy every day, but the injury did not respond to treatment. With my two weeks' 'leave' up, I telephoned Pieter to tell him I needed to stay an extra week for more treatment and he objected. 'You must come back to Stellenbosch now. You have to train. You have a lot of work to do.' It was the first time in my life that anything had prevented me from running and I felt helpless. Tablets, cortisone injections and physiotherapy – nothing worked.

It was left to my friend Elizna van Zyl to reveal Pieter's plans when, visiting me at my sister Cara's house, she let slip that my coach was planning to leave Stellenbosch. 'Are you going to Saldanha Bay?' she wanted to know. In response to my blank look she told me Pieter had applied for a teaching post there and it was the final straw. After all we had been through I couldn't believe he would do something like that without telling me and I was bitterly disappointed. My whole life revolved around Pieter and I had been prepared to stick with him no matter what. Had he said 'You are going to Japan', I would have gone, but I would be left to fend for myself if he moved to Saldanha Bay.

Still horrified, I rang Jannie and told him I didn't want to stay in Stellenbosch any longer. He came to see me and we decided that I would, as I had planned, spend a lot more time in England. It made sense to me because up until then I had been torn apart. Pieter had wanted me in Stellenbosch, I had to remain loyal to Britain and I wanted to see my family. It couldn't continue and the best solution was to move permanently to England and spend my holidays in Bloemfontein.

As a result of my decision, Andy Norman flew out and we had a meeting at Graham's house in Stellenbosch at which Jannie, Andy, Graham, Pieter and I were present. What it boiled down to was that Pieter would no longer be closely involved in my career and I would stay permanently in England where, Andy suggested, Harry Wilson should coach me. Selecting Harry, a top British coach, had been Andy's idea and when it became obvious during the meeting that Pieter was unlikely to play an active role in my career, he got up and walked out of the room. It was the end and I felt cut in half. When he closed the door he severed everything that had existed between us, and although I saw him afterwards things would never again be the same.

Our final encounter before I headed back overseas was in Bloemfontein in December, when Pieter was attending the South African University championships. We bumped into each other at the track, where I was a spectator, and later had what was to be our final face to face conversation. I had spoken to Pieter on the phone following the 'walk out' in Stellenbosch and he had sent me a training programme, but I could sense at this last meeting that our relationship could never be repaired. Too much water had passed under the bridge and I got the impression that Pieter, who was now coaching some good athletes such as Elizna van Zyl, was bored with me. Although he gave me another programme

130

in Bloemfontein, along with the advice to 'forget the leg', Pieter appeared more interested in telling me how well Elizna was performing than he was with my problems. Elizna's progress was the focus of Pieter's attention when I rang him subsequent to our chat in Bloemfontein and, like two ships that passed in the night, we lost contact over that festive season and an era ended.

The new era dawned with my determination to fight back from the injury and recapture my winning form, but I wasn't yet ready to live on my own in Guildford. I asked my friend, Minke van der Walt, to stay with me while I found my feet and when she accepted, matters were settled as far as Graham and Jannie were concerned. I was to have a new coach in Harry Wilson and I would live in England . . . everything was fine, problem solved. I wish it had been that easy.

14
Doctor's Orders

I went back to Guildford in January 1987 with Minke van der Walt, whom I had met through my good friend Miensie Roux. I was pleased to have her with me because, after making the final break with Pieter, I was vulnerable and lonely. Minke's expenses were met by the Trust and we settled down in Guildford while I attempted to pick up the pieces of a training schedule that had been shattered by the leg injury.

I made another friend in Guildford, aspiring musician Mark Davies, who was to be a tower of strength later on, when things really started going wrong. Minke and I met Mark in a tea-shop, where I proved conclusively that I was the champion tea-drinker in all of England. Mark thought he was good at knocking back a good many cups of tea, but I was better and drank him under the table on that day. Together, we were to become experts on the tea-shops of Surrey and Greater London. I am so fond of the beverage that I always keep half-a-dozen varieties on hand in my kitchen to cater for the taste of any visitors I might receive: South African herbal tea, or Rooibos, Earl Grey, jasmine tea . . . I've got them all.

Two days after meeting Mark, I left for West Germany

with Minke to go to a clinic in Freiburg where there was a doctor who had a reputation for being one of the best sports medicine men in the world. My leg had not responded to any of the treatment I had received in South Africa and England and, being unable to run in comfort or stretch properly, I was getting desperate. The German doctor had been recommended to me by an athlete friend of mine in Bloemfontein, javelin-thrower Koos van der Merwe, and I arrived in Freiburg full of hope. I had difficulty understanding the clinic staff because they spoke very little English and for the first four days I had a series of injections, which made me terribly tired, and scans. I just wanted to sleep the days away, but I perked up when the doctor told me that I could start running again.

I went back to Minke in the hotel with the good news and went for a run the next morning. Although the leg didn't feel too bad when I went out for my first run following the injections, I still couldn't stretch, but I left Freiburg more hopeful than I had been for weeks.

Back in England, Andy Norman organized a press conference where it was announced that Harry Wilson would be my new coach; but though Pieter and I had effectively split up at the end of 1986, I still felt bad about the whole situation. It is impossible to erase the memory of a coach who has guided you through six years and I had not yet confirmed to Pieter that Harry would take over. Pieter must have assumed that, as I had not been running, I had no coach, and I felt sorry for him that he had to hear about Harry's involvement in a newscast instead of from me personally.

Joining Harry's squad put me in a tricky situation, because he had not been my choice in the first place. He was a fine coach, one of the best, but it had been Andy Norman who had selected Harry as the best man to get Zola back into winning shape. Given time, I might well have asked Harry to take me on, but under the circumstances it was almost impossible for me to form any kind of relationship with him and I was taken aback when, at my first training session with him, at Woking, he asked, 'Why did you choose me?' I was under the impression that Andy, who wielded considerable power in British athletics, had briefed Harry, and I had no answer other than a shrug of the shoulders. I couldn't tell Harry that I had not had any say in picking a coach and when he asked me what had happened to Pieter I burst into tears.

It was my fault that Harry and I got off to such a bad start, but I couldn't bring myself to be honest with him and tell him straight out what had happened. It would have been insulting for a man with his reputation to hear from an athlete already steeped in controversy that he had basically been pulled out of a hat. I let the matter rest and trained with Harry again the next day, when my leg started playing up.

Harry put me on to one of the physiotherapists who attended the British team and again there was a personality clash. I didn't like the physiotherapist's approach and he had no answer for three vital questions: (a) what was wrong; (b) what to do about it; and (c) how to prevent it from recurring.

Back I went to the German clinic with Minke, where the doctors told me that I had trained too hard too quickly. Again, the treatment had little effect and with no concrete evidence that the injury was responding I returned to Guildford and faced up to the fact that I would probably never run again.

Out of sight meant out of mind to the people who were supposedly looking after my affairs. My family were in Bloemfontein; Jannie didn't seem interested in me when I wasn't winning races; and I only heard from Graham once every few weeks. If I wasn't running it seemed that nobody cared what happened to me and, although I had Minke staying with me and the friendship of Mark, I could feel the loneliness closing in. Even the British officials and promoters ignored me though the previous year I had been in great demand. Andy Norman stayed clear of me, as did Les Jones, and I started getting desperate.

What was the use, I wondered, of staying in England when I couldn't run? I knew I was injured, but nobody seemed to care. The phone stopped ringing, there were no knocks on the door, and I told Minke that I wanted to return to South Africa in April. Minke, however, employed some delaying tactics by talking to Mark's brother Tom, who came round for tea and did a quick selling job on the idea of a two-week break at the holiday resort of Lanzarote in the Canary Islands.

Desperate to escape the isolation brought about by my injury, it was an offer I couldn't refuse and the three of us, Minke, Tom, and I, headed off in search of sun and fun.

Before we left I remember watching the world cross-country championships on television. It was a nasty experience knowing that, had I been fit, I could probably have made it a hat-trick. Under normal circumstances, if you cannot compete in a specific race for any particular reason, you can always go out and put in a hard training session: it helps relieve the frustration. But in 1987 I couldn't even do that because of my leg. I was restricted to swimming and I spent a lot of time in the water at Lanzarote, with the result that the muscles in my shoulders began developing and my shirts started getting tight as I filled out.

What a pleasure it was to have the use of an Olympic-size pool at Lanzarote after the tiny pool I had been using in Guildford! The break was just what I needed and I loved Lanzarote, with its mysterious, dark rocks and soil. The very earth seemed to be alive compared to the sodden English countryside, and it was invigorating riding and swimming in such intriguing surroundings.

We had drama on our arrival when Minke retrieved her suitcase at the airport to discover that it had split open in

135

transit and her clothes had been soiled. But we righted that quickly enough with a shopping spree the following day, before getting down to the serious business of relaxing and enjoying ourselves.

I was surprised to see in Lanzarote the German doctor who had treated me at Freiburg. He rebuked me for not returning to the clinic for more treatment, but he gave me more injections and advised me against riding which, he said, would aggravate the injury (which he still could not pin-point).

The only dampener on my holiday came when I entered a triathlon and during the first leg, swimming, noticed that the pool area had suddenly become quiet. Tom pulled me out of the water and I saw that one of the holiday-makers, a man, had suffered a heart attack in the pool. To make matters worse, his daughter was present – it was she who had pulled him to the side -- and although the people around him did all they could, including mouth-to-mouth resuscitation, they could not save him and he died at the pool side.

After that, I didn't much feel like using the swimming pool and instead went to the lagoon. But the water there was so filthy that I put the macabre scene I had witnessed earlier out of my mind and returned to the pool.

Unwinding in Lanzarote was just what the doctor – figuratively, not literally, because none of the 'real' doctors I saw could do anything for my injury – ordered and this was the most peaceful period I had experienced since leaving Bloemfontein.

Apart from the physical exercise we were getting, the food was lovely, although sometimes a little off-putting. Like the time Tom ordered squid, squashed his knife against one of the legs and withdrew it with a tentacle stuck firmly to the blade!

I was a different young woman when I returned to England, to be met at the airport by Mark, who presented me with a bouquet of yellow flowers, and his father, Tom.

136

The warm weather had followed us across the Channel and I felt a lot better for the short break. Summer was on the way, which meant I could do some gardening with Minke's mother, who had come to visit, and another welcome visitor was Graham.

Graham came to England just after the South African general election and I was very pleased to see him. But while Graham kept a low profile, Janine was very much part of the political arena as Denis Worrall's campaign manager when the former South African ambassador to the Court of St James stood as an Independent against Constitutional Minister Chris Heunis, and I started having second thoughts about my association with him. It was important for me to be apolitical and no matter which party Jannie supported – the Nationalists, the Conservatives, the Peoples' Federal Party or the Independents – I didn't want it to rub off on me.

I had a long talk with Graham, telling him of my plans to go to college in England and how my leg was still preventing me from doing any meaningful training. We also discussed my relationship with Pieter at length and came to the conclusion that part of the problem was his apparent inability to say three things – please, thank you, and I'm sorry. I also briefed Graham on my unsatisfactory relationship with Harry Wilson, conceding that once I had made a full recovery perhaps things might work out better.

The other subject we covered was delicate – my relationship with Minke. We were not getting along very well and it wasn't surprising. All Minke had to occupy herself with was my welfare and the time had come for us to part. It wasn't her fault – we had a personality clash – and I asked Graham to find another place for me to stay: somewhere where I could be more independent.

The worst part was confronting Minke, who was obviously frustrated by her 'baby-sitting' job and very homesick. But we had a long talk and I was frank with her when I told her it would be better for us to part. The truth was that I really did want to be more independent. I wanted to get back into international athletics, and, even if I had to rest the leg for twelve months, it would be worth it in the long run.

I packed in preparation for my trip to South Africa to spend my twenty-first birthday with my family. The car, a Peugeot, had been given to me as part of an endorsement deal, but I had to return it in 1987. In the world of sports business you are only as good as your current performances and Peugeot had no compunction in taking the car back. Forget the injury, it was results they wanted and no results meant no car.

Nobody apart from Cara knew that I was coming home early for my birthday and I had immense fun ringing Estelle from Jan Smuts airport. 'I wish I could see you', I said plaintively. 'Don't worry,' said Estelle. 'It's your birthday soon and we'll see you then.' I also phoned Ma, but she had been tipped off by Cara and played along with me, although we kept Estelle in the dark. Those 'in the know' prepared a huge welcoming dinner for me in Bloemfontein and I hid when Estelle arrived at the house. She was so surprised to see me when I popped out that she started crying.

It was marvellous to be back at home with my family and I made the most of it. Being with Ma, Estelle, Cara and Quintus made all the difference, and it was great seeing old friends again. Still unable to run effectively I was soon back in the pool in Bloemfontein, although the water was a freezing 17°C. It was so cold I felt numb and on one day there was mist rising from the water which reminded me of a swamp in a James Bond movie.

My flirtation with swimming had begun in the latter part of 1986 after the break-up with Pieter. I could barely keep afloat at that stage, but my friend Marinda Botha took me to the university pool and taught me how to swim. We didn't have university passes so we sometimes sneaked into the pool area at night and it was very scary in the dark. The first time only one side of the pool was lit and I did one length, which was a real achievement for me at that stage. But, when I got to the end of the pool it was so dark that my imagination ran riot. Novices are always uneasy in deep water and in my mind I started hearing the theme tune from *Jaws*. What was lurking beneath the surface, waiting to pull me down? I took fright and splashed back to the shallow end in a time an Olympian would have been proud of!

On another night, when it was really warm, Marinda and I with a friend from school, Jacques Burger, whom I used to do a lot of training with when I was in Bloemfontein, crept into the pool at the Technikon; without any lighting, we couldn't see the colour of the water. I dived in and it tasted bitter – it must have been really green – but we stuck it out. Like me, Jacques was not a strong swimmer and we were splashing around when we saw him going up and down, up and down, I thought he was playing the fool and it was only when he reached the side and frantically hauled himself out that we found out he had been on the verge of drowning.

No amount of swimming could, however, compensate for the frustration of not being able to run properly. I felt literally hamstrung, like a Formula One motor-racing driver who had blown the engine of his car on the warm-up of the first Grand Prix of the season, and I was intrigued to receive a telephone call from Bloemfontein coach Leon Botha. 'Listen Zola,' he said a week before my twenty-first birthday, 'I have just spoken to Fanie van Zijl and he thinks you should see an applied kinesiologist, Dr Ronald Holder, in Johannesburg. He's the man who helped Fanie get over the terrible injury problem that threatened to put him into a wheelchair.' I knew of Fanie: every athlete in the country did. He had been one of South Africa's greatest middle distance runners and was now a very successful businessman in Randfontein. Ready to try anything, I contacted Fanie and arranged to meet him in Johannesburg the following day, where he would take me to see the man I was to refer to as 'the Doctor'.

139

Jannie was in Bloemfontein at the time and I rang him to ask for the money I needed to purchase an air ticket to Jan Smuts. Jannie agreed to give me the money, but advised me against getting involved with Fanie. I have never discovered why, but there is bad blood between those two men, and Jannie was adamant I should have nothing to do with Fanie. With so much apparent ill-feeling between the pair, I decided it would be better for me to pay my own way to Johannesburg and I refunded the money I got from Jannie and bought my own ticket.

Still confused by Jannie's obvious antagonism, I got cold feet next morning and rang Fanie to tell him I had changed my mind. Instead of going swimming as I usually did, I was at home in my flat when I received a telephone call from Ma. Hearing that I had decided against seeing this mysterious doctor, she took matters into her own hands and rang Fanie herself. Fanie made it clear that Ronald Holder was probably the only man in the world who could help me. He had cured Fanie and had a long list of South Africa's top athletes on his books. He was my last chance. 'What about it, Zola?' prodded Ma. 'Give it a try.'

It was to prove a momentous decision and off I went to Johannesburg. Fanie's concern at that stage was purely philanthropic. He had heard I had a problem and he believed the Doctor could solve it. Waiting for him at Jan Smuts was tricky as I had no idea what Fanie looked like. Finally I saw a balding man wearing glasses and carrying a Nike bag. He looked athletic and he turned out to be the man I was waiting for.

Fanie introduced me to his charming wife, Corrie, a keen cross-country runner with whom I immediately established a strong bond of friendship, and told me all about Dr Ronald Holder. The man worked miracles, said Fanie, and he did it all on the principle of balancing the body through the use of orthotics, or wedges, in the shoes and a series of

140

exercises. The wedges were made from the pages of a telephone book; the treatment was so precise that one page made a difference. The Doctor, said Fanie, came from a chiropractic background but had branched out into applied kinetics because he was ahead of his time and his results were remarkable.

I met the Doctor on 18 May 1987 – a day which I shall never forget as it marked the start of my recovery, thanks to this wonderful man. Much of the Doctor's work involves testing the body to find the muscular imbalances that can cause injury. The feet, he explains, are the foundations of the body, just like the foundations of a house, and if the foundations are not stable neither is the structure they support.

The Doctor tested me and pin-pointed a muscular imbalance which required a thick wedge and when I ran 4 kilometres that evening, the pain had miraculously diminished. I saw the Doctor again the following day and returned to Bloemfontein in exultation. It was wonderful to run without pain – I was even able, for the first time in weeks, to sleep through the night without being woken by the throbbing – and it was all due to the Doctor. He had succeeded where a host of specialists and physiotherapists had failed.

Being able to run freely again was the best birthday present anybody could have given to me, and after I turned twenty-one I visited the Doctor every week in Johannesburg. As the wedges corrected muscle imbalance they had to be changed and that required constant testing and a strict regime of exercises and sometimes excruciatingly painful massage.

Fanie's involvement in my career became more pronounced with each visit I made to Johannesburg, because I stayed with him and his family. Graham and Jannie were not really interested in my problems at that stage and Fanie was the only person prepared to help a desperate young woman who was afraid her career was about to come

141

crashing down unless the Doctor worked his magic.

When they realized just how close I was getting to Fanie, Graham and Jannie began giving me a hard time. I received countless telephone calls from Graham, urging me to return to England because I was spending far too much time in South Africa. What Graham did not understand was that I had finally found somebody who could cure my injury. With the wedges changing frequently, I was dependent on the Doctor and I saw no point in going back to England when I couldn't compete. I was unfit and over-weight and I needed the Doctor's treatment and Fanie's coaching to get back into shape.

Fanie was then a tower of strength and nothing was too much trouble. He opened his house to me, fetched me from the airport, took me to the Doctor and attended to my every need. When he came to Bloemfontein with his family we agreed that he would become my coach, although as far as the outside world was concerned his only role was as a liaison man between me and the Doctor.

When I compared the assistance I was getting from Fanie to Jannie's involvement in my career, I decided the time had come to say goodbye to Jannie: I was getting no help from him. So I did the decent thing and wrote him a letter, dated 18 July 1987:

Dear Uncle Jannie

Firstly I would like to say thank you for your assistance and aid over the last two years. Thank you very much, it is very much appreciated.

Circumstances over the past two months have changed a lot and I have now, after long deliberation, decided to write this letter to you. I have decided to be more self-reliant from now onwards and more independent. It is therefore that I would like to thank you for your

142

help and aid over the past times but would prefer to be standing on my own two legs in future. Circumstances have also changed so that your capacity as adviser and manager will no longer be required. It is very important for me to be self-reliant and to make my own decisions in future. Yet it is not the end of the friendship and your friendship will be appreciated in future.

Another factor is your involvement with Denis Worrall's election campaign. This had made circumstances very difficult for me in England and I did not want to become involved in politics.

I would like to talk with you in future. Will you please be so kind as to forward to me a copy of my account in Stellenbosch, as well as of my Trust.

This letter is written in the hope that you will regard it as sincere and it was written in a spirit of friendship. It is the end of your involvement as adviser and manager but not of our friendship. I hope that your understanding of my independence and self-reliance means as much to you as your friendship for me.

Love
Zola

Jannie's reply, sent by registered mail on 28 July was:

Dear Zola

With this I wish to acknowledge your letter dated 18 July 1987.

After full consultation with the other members of the Zola Budd Sports Trust, I must tell you that the Trust plans to continue its responsibilities until 19 November 1988.

Two members of the Trust, being myself and Mr Graham Boonzaier, will be in Britain from 24 August 1987 and would like to discuss the whole issue with you together with Mr Victor Washtell of Touche Ross.

With friendly wishes,
Oom Jannie

To this, I replied on 6 August:

Dear Uncle Jannie,

I hereby acknowledge receipt of your letter dated 28 July 1987.

It is with regret that I must inform you that I intend keeping to my letter dated 18 July 1987. In your full consultation as mentioned in your letter, with the other members of the Trust, Mr P Labuschagne and Mr G Boonzaier, it came to my attention that there was not consensus amongst the Trust members.

I intend to consult with Mr G Boonzaier as soon as possible after my return to Britain to discuss my future plans. I believe that I myself, either with the help of Mr Boonzaier or Mr Washtell, will be able to discuss all aspects personally.

Regarding the Trust, I must inform you that I do not regard the contract as legally binding as a result of various obvious reasons and in future I will talk only with Mr G Boonzaier about any private or financial matters.

With friendly greetings,
Zola Budd

It was the end of another era, but the start of an equally traumatic period, as Fanie hitched up to a Buddwagon that was rapidly running out of steam.

145

15
The Whole Truth

Brakpan and Randfontein: two towns in South Africa whose names were to reverberate through the athletics world as the the IAAF set out on their witchhunt in an attempt to force the British Amateur Athletic Board to suspend me for twelve months. On 24 March 1988 I was suspended until the IAAF council meeting on 15 April of that year, where the council would consider if I had contravened rule 53(1), which declares ineligible for competition any person who has 'taken part in any athletics meeting or event in which any of the competitors were, to his (her) knowledge, ineligible to compete under the IAAF rules'. On 15 April the council deferred a decision to an inner caucus and the following day the IAAF recommended unanimously to the British Board that I be banned for twelve months for 'at least being in breach of the spirit of the rules of the IAAF'. 'It is', they said, 'the view that the BAAB ought to consider a suspension for the athlete from competition for twelve months.'

Did I take part in a cross-country race in Brakpan? Did I hand out the prizes after the New Year's Eve race in Randfontein? The answer is 'No' on both counts, but for IAAF, which can be swayed in Council by the voting power of its African and Asian members, many of whom are rigidly opposed to anything South African, the incidents gave them all the ammunition they needed to recommend a suspension.

When I became a British national and ran in Los Angeles there were howls of protest from many anti-apartheid quarters and, taking the composition of the IAAF Council into consideration, I had little chance of receiving a sympathetic hearing when the case concerning my alleged participation at Brakpan came before them.

The ball that was to bowl me out of international competition was started rolling by African member countries of the IAAF, who were threatening a boycott of the 1988 world cross-country championships in Auckland. The IAAF asked the British Amateur Athletic Board to withdraw me from the team for the championships and the BAAB refused, saying: 'In the light that no evidence has been forthcoming from the IAAF concerning Miss Budd's activities in South Africa in 1987 and her assurances concerning the allegations made, the BAAB consider that the IAAF must, if they require her to be de-selected, instruct the BAAB to de-select her.'

I withdrew from the cross-country championships on 16 March rather than jeopardize the chances of my British team-mates, but the IAAF persisted in their attempt to prove that I had contravened the rules and Council's conclusion that I had broken the 'spirit' of the rules was not surprising considering the spread of votes.

It became apparent in 1984 that African members of the IAAF perceived me as a symbol of South Africa and of apartheid and among the twenty-three Council members in 1988 was Senegal's Lamine Diack, president of the African Amateur Athletic Confederation. With forty-eight members in seven zones and, therefore, forty-eight votes, Diack carried a lot of clout, particularly if he voted the same way as Essa Al-Dashti, a Council member and senior vice-president of the Asian AAA. Asia's forty-one votes and Africa's forty-eight gave those two continents eighty-nine of the Council's 181 votes and it was clear after a five-hour sitting of the Council that my fate was sealed. *The Independent* of 16 April 1988, quotes Al-Dashti as saying 'It will go very bad for Budd' and adds that he shook his head when asked if I would ever run again. Diack and Al-Dashti could, therefore, sway any meeting from the onset and if anti-South African sentiment played any part in my suspension, it is worth noting that Europe's thirty-five votes includes countries such as the Soviet Union, East Germany, Romania and Czechoslovakia, none of which could be expected to look favourably on a woman who was widely regarded as having used Britain as a passport of convenience. In addition, the North and Central American vote of thirty-two includes Jamaica, Cuba and Trinidad, all known opponents of apartheid.

For the record, I offer my account of the two incidents in question.

In 1987 I was occasionally staying with and being trained by former South African middle distance star Fanie van Zijl, who had introduced me to applied kinesiologist Dr Ronald Holder. Fanie's wife, Corrie, and son, Stephan, were both keen runners and as I was staying with the family while being treated by Doctor Holder, it was natural that I should watch them in action during the cross-country season.

The first of five races at which I was present, but in which I did not take part, was on 6 June in Brakpan. According to my training diary, I ran 10 kilometres in the morning in 41 minutes and in the afternoon went with Fanie and his family to the cross-country. I was wearing my training kit and after I had watched Stephan's race, Fanie told me to run two laps on the outskirts of the course. Well aware of the potential danger of being connected to any athletic event in South Africa, I was reluctant to do so, because, as a British runner, I was afraid it could cause trouble. In the past I had watched some of my friends running cross-country, but had never dared run in the vicinity. On this occasion I had a bad feeling. 'I don't think it's a good

148

idea', I told Fanie. 'Don't worry,' he replied, aware that I was not happy about the idea. 'Nothing will happen. Just stay on the outskirts of the course.'

So off I went on a 20-minute run, sticking to the outside of the course and keeping well clear of the start and finishing areas. I was training, pure and simple, and, although I did run on a short section of the course, I certainly wasn't taking part in the race. I remember overtaking a few men competing in the veterans' category, but it was all completely innocent. Mixed races are not permitted under the IAAF rules anyway, and I didn't run past the start or finish. My training finished, I watched Corrie's race and we all went home.

The fateful New Year's Eve race, organized by Fanie, was just as innocent. I had wanted to go to Bloemfontein to welcome in the New Year, but the idea seemed to upset Fanie, and Corrie came to me 'on the quiet' in the role of a peacemaker. 'After all he's done for you, Fanie thinks you should support his race,' she said. That made me feel guilty, so I stayed in Randfontein and went with the van Zijl family to the race that bore Fanie's name. One of Fanie's drivers took my bike to the race venue in a bakkie and, dressed in khaki shorts, a white shirt and Nike shoes, I rode around the course, following the race and enjoying the action on the road. One of the race marshals even tried to pull me off the road because I was riding on the course, but he allowed me to proceed when he recognized me.

Later, at the prize-giving, I was watching Corrie present the awards when I was suddenly called to the rostrum over the public address system. It was the first I knew about it and I couldn't stand there without responding. As far as I was aware, nobody apart from the van Zijls knew I was present but, unable to snub Fanie by staying put, I went to the rostrum and a young girl handed me three yellow roses. Some black members of the crowd became quite excited when they saw me and started chanting my name, but Fanie simply thanked me for being at the race and it was all over.

There were a few pressmen around who chatted to me afterwards, but, aware of the danger of being associated with a race in South Africa, I declined to pose for a photograph with the winners. The journalists could not understand why I was so reserved and they didn't like it when Fanie came along and stopped them from asking me some politically sensitive questions. They were obviously annoyed because neither Fanie nor I was being particularly helpful, but I was able to escape when I saw Sonja Laxton, one of South Africa's greatest women athletes, and her husband Ian, and we went off for a chat.

After that, Minette, Stephan and I got into Fanie's car and we went to a roadhouse for a hamburger. Because Fanie was the race organizer and needed to be on the route, he had a blue flashing light on the car roof and we drove through Randfontein looking like a plain-clothes police patrol. The flashing light ensured that we got prompt service at the roadhouse and I went to bed as soon as we got back to Fanie's house, as I faced the long drive to Bloemfontein the following day.

16
Gunned Down

After training with Fanie for three months from May 1987, when he introduced me to Dr Ronald Holder, I went to England with my mother in August, unaware that just nine months later my athletics dreams would be shattered by the determination of the IAAF to make me a scapegoat for apartheid. With the Doctor's help, I was again mobile, the stress fracture where my right hamstring joined the pelvis responding to treatment. The wedges were doing their work, correcting the muscle imbalances in my body which caused the injury in the first place and I was anxious to test myself in competition after a long lay-off.

We selected a 5 kilometres handicap at Hyde Park on 4 September for my 'comeback' and I was feeling great as I drove to London with my mother and Mark, who had become a good friend and would be a tower of strength the following year when the IAAF was gunning for me and Fanie, who had other commitments, left me to fend for myself. It was nice being back in England, and Minke van der Walt had done a super job at the house. She had redecorated, and it was lovely and cozy. Even better, Minke and I were back on good terms after the personality clashes of the previous year and we were all in high spirits.

The apprehension I felt at the start of the race quickly

151

evaporated as I concentrated on doing what I did best – running – and I was pleased with my time of 16:13. It was wonderful to run without pain and I was confident that my career was about to take an upward turn. Tired and happy, I celebrated my first race in more than twelve months with pizza, ice cream and apple pie and later went to the theatre with Ma and Mark.

Next on the agenda was a two-mile cross-country event at Horsham, where I did myself a lot more harm than good by attempting to take part incognito. I wanted to keep a low profile and Mark and I selected the Horsham race because it was close to Guildford and I could enter on the line. That was a big attraction, because with no pre-entries, nobody would know I was there. The fanfare that usually greeted a Zola Budd race would be missing and I could concentrate on the job in hand. The last thing I wanted was pressure – the press would have rolled up in droves had they been given advance notice that I was competing, along with the inevitable demonstrators – and I thought I could escape detection by entering the race using an alias.

But, by using the assumed name of 'Miss T Davies', who was actually Mark's sister Tamara, I was looking for trouble. England's hard-nosed pressmen soon got wind of what had happened: they had a field day exposing who Miss Davies really was. Any thoughts I had of getting away with the pretence backfired almost immediately. The organizers recognized me and I was told that if I intended running under an assumed name I would not qualify for prize money. That was fine by me: I wasn't there for the money anyway, and I won the race in 10:24; another satisfactory performance, but one which antagonized Fanie when he heard about my attempted deception.

'You should have known better,' he admonished me when he arrived in England. 'What made you do a silly thing like that?' My only defence was that it seemed logical at the time. Two years later, I was still able to get a chuckle out of the incident, because fan mail addressed to 'Miss T Davies' was still arriving.

This time, the post-race 'celebration dinner' took place at a really tacky eater, where Mark and I had fish 'n' chips, and I horrified my well-brought-up English friend by dunking my bread in the tea. That just wasn't done in England, but I laughed at Mark and told him it was accepted practice in South Africa with rusks, a traditional Afrikaans type of biscuit.

Mark was still recovering from a training run in the woods the previous day when, jogging through unfamiliar territory, we got lost under my 'expert' direction. Salvation seemed in sight when he saw a man walking with two dogs, but he must have been afraid we were muggers. He looked ready to lash out with his walking stick when Mark approached him, and then one dog attacked Mark, biting him on the ankle. With Mark hobbling on a foot that was swelling rapidly, we beat a hasty retreat, found our bearings and headed for the nearest hospital, where we spent hours waiting for Mark to have the wound cleaned and a tetanus injection.

Being attacked by dogs is an occupational hazard for an athlete doing road or cross-country work – top South African ultra-distance runner Helen Lucre was savaged quite badly by a bull terrier in 1988 while out on a training run – and I was fortunate to escape injury on that day in the woods.

My mother went home after spending two weeks in England – she had the time of her life on this trip which made up for all her unhappiness in 1984, when she had such a hard time from my father and I walked out of the house – and Fanie came over for a week in which I did a lot of good training.

It was quite an experience shopping for clothes with Fanie and Mark so that I could look smart for a business meeting I had with my accountant, Victor Washtell, and Graham Boonzaier. I have never bothered myself with

153

clothes – a shirt and trousers are good enough for me – and I never wore make-up. Now, for the first time in my life, I was shopping for things like nail varnish and I bought smart trousers and a shirt, which I hoped would make me presentable.

The meeting revolved around money and my agreement with Graham, Pieter and Jannie Momberg. I wanted to get out of the Zola Budd Sports Trust agreement I had signed in 1984 and Graham wanted to square the books as far as the bridging finance he had provided was concerned. That related to things like my travel costs and those of Carin and Pieter and my various friends who had come to England to train with me during the period I was involved with Jannie and Pieter.

Graham's solution was to take fifteen per cent of my income from endorsements, contracts and appearance money, but I wanted to make a clean break and pay him outright. Among the monies owing to Graham was an amount of £25,000 – the Trust's cut from the huge fee of £90,000 that Graham negotiated for the re-match with Mary Decker in 1985. The agreement then, for a race which gained me more enemies than anything else apart from the fact that I was born in South Africa, was that two cheques would be issued. One, for £25,000, was to go to the Trust established by Graham, Jannie and Pieter, and the other, for the balance, would be paid into my official British Athlete's Fund. As it turned out, only one cheque, for the whole amount, was issued and Victor agreed at the meeting in September 1987 that I could make a loan against my British fund to repay Graham. The balance of what I owed would only be paid when I received invoices from Graham and I had no idea of how much was involved.

It was with a sigh of relief on my part that Graham and I reached agreement. I was anxious to close the chapter on that period of my life and I had already broken off with Jannie, writing to thank him for his help and to say I no longer required his services. I was to see Jannie for the last time in October 1987 at the Airport Holiday Inn in Johannesburg, and it was not a pleasant experience. Fanie was with me and I could almost smell the antagonism between Fanie and Jannie. They disliked each other and I ended up having a row with Jannie, who gave me a lecture on keeping my name out of the South African newspapers. 'I get a bad press no matter what I do,' I told him as he and Fanie squared up to each other like two angry bulls. 'If I have the chance to get some good publicity, I'm going to take it.'

Although Jannie was no longer connected with my career, I was very sad our relationship had to end this way. There had been many good times with the man I called 'Uncle', although he had made me uncomfortable at times by making no attempt to hide his South African background, with the 1985 world cross-country championships a case in point.

Sorting out the money side of my career with Victor and Graham proved to be relatively simple compared to breaking off with Harry Wilson. Within a week of his arrival in England, Fanie told me I had to leave Harry and it was a task that both distressed me and made me feel ashamed. My only defence is that I had not picked Harry in the first place, but there can be no denying that I used him as a front man when Fanie took over my training. Because I had put all my trust in Fanie, I did what I was told and arranged a meeting with Harry at which I was to drop my bombshell.

At twenty-one I suppose I could have thought and acted for myself, yet I was once again dependent on a man whom I believed was the only person who could get me back into international athletics. Part of my reliance on Fanie hinged on the Doctor, because it was through Fanie I had met the Doctor, and Fanie and the Doctor were close. Fanie was my link to the Doctor and the Doctor's treatment was just as vital to me as Fanie's guidance and coaching. If Fanie said 'Jump', I jumped,

155

and when Fanie said 'Get rid of Harry', I did what I was told.

I arranged to have lunch with Harry at a place near Harpenden and the deception started when Fanie drove me there and then sat in a café across the road while I told Harry I wanted to be more independent and didn't need a coach on a day-to-day basis. It was awful not being able to tell Harry the truth, and he suspected that Fanie was more deeply involved than simply as a go-between for the Doctor and me.

It was all such a farce and I wished I had the courage to defy Fanie and say straight out, 'Harry, I don't need you any more. I have Fanie coaching me.' Instead, I pussy-footed around the subject, telling Harry that if I needed his advice I would contact him. I don't blame him for getting angry, although I was annoyed at the way Harry subsequently castigated me in the press.

My mistake was not ending the relationship there and then and it wasn't fair for a man with Harry's reputation as a top coach to have a twenty-one-year-old athlete giving him the big brush-off. But I was still unable to stand firmly on my own two feet at that stage and, like Pieter before him, I regarded Fanie as essential to my athletic advancement.

With Harry gone, I still needed a British coach for the sake of appearances and when Fanie returned to England from a business trip to America we had a meeting with British officials Andy Norman and Les Jones. They agreed that Harry would not have worked out anyway – no top coach could be expected to tolerate somebody else behind the scenes and having Fanie in the background would have been more than Harry could stand – and they were quite happy when I suggested John Bryant as a 'front man'.

If British Amateur Athletic Board officials accepted that Fanie could continue coaching me on the quiet, it was good enough for me, and Fanie and I approached John Bryant with the proposal. Since I had first met him in 1984, when he was a member of the *Daily Mail*'s 'Get Zola' squad,

John and I had become friends. He had since moved to the *Independent*, but he was a runner himself who knew quite a lot about coaching. Fanie and I were perfectly honest with John, telling him that I needed an English coach to give me legitimacy while Fanie did the 'real' work behind the scenes. Because he was a true friend, John agreed.

My second major problem solved, Fanie and I started looking for a suitable race and, after paging through *Athletics Weekly*, decided on the 10-mile Kodak Classic at Bangor on 19 September. It turned out to be Bangor, Northern Ireland not Bangor, Wales, as we had first thought, but we rang Les Jones and he made all the arrangements.

The Kodak Classic was by far the most important race since my return to Britain in 1987 and the familiar butterflies began fluttering in my stomach beforehand. Would the leg stand up to it? How much of my competitive edge had I lost through the injury? The fact that I was nervous was a good sign, because it proved that even if my training had taken a knock my zest for running remained. My passion for producing a run that would satisfy my own high standards was still intact and I would not be disappointed.

Making the race easier was the absence of demonstrators, and I set off with a spirited spurt that had Fanie yelling to me to slow down after the first 3 kilometres. But I was enjoying myself and it was reflected in my running on that day. This was what it was all about! I felt the old glow of self-satisfaction when I crossed the line in 32:17 – a good time considering the long lay-off – and, looking back, I regard the Classic as one of my best post-world championship races. I proved to myself that I could still produce the goods and an added bonus was the absence of political interference.

From such a promising start in England, Fanie and I, joined by his wife Corrie and Stephan and Minette, headed for the continent and a race at Biella in Italy. This was a 3 kilometres road race and it was panic stations when I developed tummy trouble an hour before the event. The last thing I needed was to be forced to 'go' during the race, but my luck held on a course that included two steep climbs.

Among the entrants was Dutch middle distance star Elly van Hulst and I started off fast, watching her like a hawk. I still wanted revenge for a race in Belgium the previous year, when she bumped me from the inside lane to the third lane on the track, and there's nothing better than a victory for soothing the ego. We were good friends off the track – I had chatted to her after the European championships in a mixture of Afrikaans and Dutch – but that's where it stopped. In Italy I wanted very badly to beat her and it wasn't long after I had hit the front that I realized we were on the second hill. I had been so intent on keeping tabs on Elly that I hadn't even noticed the first climb and, with less than 200 metres to go, I saw Fanie. 'Come on,' he urged. 'Drop your head, lift your arms and start sprinting.' I followed instructions and the results were gratifying. This was the first top-class event I had won with a sprint for a long time and it gave my confidence a huge boost.

My reward was a trip through Europe with Fanie and his family. From Italy we went to Amsterdam and on to Germany, where I had a heart-to-heart conversation with my coach. Fanie had noticed that I was not enjoying myself as much as I should have and he asked what was upsetting me. With the memory of Pieter and Jannie still fresh in my mind, I told Fanie that I was afraid that he might also drop me if things started to go wrong. My father . . . Pieter . . . Jannie . . . Harry, I hadn't had much luck selecting people to help me through the maze of international athletics and I didn't want to get hurt again. At the back of my mind was the fact that I was beginning to notice how bombastic Fanie was, how he placed so much emphasis on making money, and it bothered me. 'You don't have to worry, Zola,' said Fanie. 'I'll never drop you.' He sounded genuine enough, but the nagging fear wouldn't go away and I cried in the shower that night as I wondered if this

158

relationship would end like the others – by going down the tubes.

From Germany we went to Switzerland, where it was lovely to see Corrie Burki again, and from there we flew back to South Africa.

Ironically, my visits to the Republic carried official British Board blessing. About a week before we went to Italy, Andy Norman and Les Jones convened a meeting at which it was agreed that my British Fund would pay for three air tickets a year to go to South Africa. Andy and Les also gave their approval to the plan that, as my 'real coach', Fanie should keep a low profile and let John Bryant appear in public.

Perhaps he knew something he wasn't telling, but Andy advised me against running in the world cross-country championships in New Zealand on 26 April the following year. Track and road, he said, were more important. 'Who will remember a cross-country champion?' he asked. 'Track gets much more attention. As far as earning money and building up your image are concerned, track is a far better proposition.'

I insisted that cross-country was good for me, but the conversation revolved around the merits of the two disciplines, with not one word from Les or Andy about possible repercussions from Third World countries over my South African links. If they suspected trouble for me in New Zealand they should have said something instead of making arrangements with Victor to increase my monthly payments to accommodate yet more South African trips.

Apart from wanting to see my family and the necessity of receiving treatment from the Doctor and re-writing an exam for my BA degree, Fanie made it clear that he expected me to train in South Africa. It was Pieter all over again as Fanie took the lead role in organizing my life. If, he argued, I wanted to be a top-class athlete, it was no good staying in Guildford. I needed to train at altitude and that meant at Randfontein with Fanie. Not even Bloemfontein

159

was good enough. Like Pieter's before him, Fanie's attitude was that to succeed I had to spend all my time with him, and that effectively scuttled my intention of living more permanently in Britain. My need to get back into the top echelon of world athletes took precedence over anything else and I went along with Fanie's plans, which included one designed to camouflage my whereabouts. Because we flew to South Africa from Switzerland and not England in October, reasoned Fanie, nobody knew where I was. If I had a telephone-answering service, and if somebody collected the mail from my Guildford home, people would think I was in England. Mark lived in Guildford . . . he could do the job.

Needless to say, the idea backfired, and I wasn't in South Africa for long when I had to go back to England anyway for just over a week, in November, to attend an athletic writers' dinner at the Park Lane Hotel.

I wanted Mark to accompany me – at that stage we were the literal version of 'just friends', although later the relationship was to end when it became more serious – but Fanie decreed otherwise. I was to go with Les Jones and his wife, tagging along without a partner, but I still had fun.

Sitting at the same table as me was the irrepressible Steve Ovett, who was a laugh a minute. He was full of jokes, but I got my own back when he asked if I was still training with ostriches in Bloemfontein. 'Oh no,' I told Steve. 'They've got bunions.'

Javelin-thrower Fatima Whitbread won the award that night but, in the middle of such a large and distinguished crowd, she looked alone. Fatima was the only British athlete to win a medal at the world championships and I could sense the animosity of the others, who had the knives out. I think it was jealousy mostly, although Fatima had also been romantically involved with Andy Norman – and he wasn't about to win any popularity contests among English athletes. I have often been lonely during my athletics career and in a way I could understand what Fatima was going

160

through, but there wasn't much I could do about it.

I was training with Mark during my lightning visit to England when, during a fartlek session one evening my left leg suddenly 'gave way'. I couldn't understand it, because it was my right leg that usually gave me trouble, but I continued my preparations for a six-mile race in Portsmouth on 15 November.

The day before the race Mark and I went for a 50-minute run and the leg went again. The quadriceps were hurting and I was reduced to a walk, but I didn't lose my sense of humour. We decided to hitch-hike back to Guildford and when nobody would give us a lift Mark lay in the road and pretended he was dead. I went into hysterics and Mark helped me to hobble back.

I rang Fanie that evening to tell him about the injury and, not realizing how bad it was, he gave me a typical coach's advice: 'Take two anti-inflammatory tablets and don't worry too much.'

I changed the wedges in my shoes, but running the race proved to be a big mistake. I developed blisters after two miles and the leg gave way at four. I was hobbling after five miles and miraculously won the event in 32:56 – a surprisingly good time considering how much I was hurting. My leg was so sore that I struggled to get out of the car before the prize-giving and with something seriously wrong, I knew I had to see the Doctor as soon as possible. I went back to Guildford that night and was on the plane the following day.

Fanie got a fright when he saw me limping down the stairs at Jan Smuts Airport and we went straight to the Doctor, who tested me and gave me new wedges. When, after three days, it became apparent that I was in real trouble, the Doctor took emergency action. The three of us went to Helpmekaar High School every second day and I ran 400-metre repetitions, stopping after each lap so that the Doctor could test me and change the wedges until we established a pattern. It was possibly the worst time of my

161

athletic career; I couldn't imagine anything being as sore as this, but I persevered.

The Doctor explained that my left leg had gone wrong as a result of the original injury to my right leg. I had over-compensated, and it was going to take a lot of time and effort to correct the imbalance.

I went to Bloemfontein for Christmas and it was exciting driving 'home' in a car laden with gifts. But I still couldn't run properly and, because I was limping, ended up training in the veld on the university campus so that nobody would see me. A run on Christmas Day proved to be disastrous and in despair I phoned Fanie. 'You had better come back,' he told me, 'and we'll see the Doctor.'

I flew up on Boxing Day and the three of us spent hours in the rain at Helpmekaar, running, being tested, changing the wedges and running again.

Even though Fanie was a tremendous help, I still had reservations. Where Pieter was quiet, Fanie was loud; worst of all, he used to shout at me. The last thing I needed in the middle of a session of hill work was to have somebody yelling at me and when I complained Fanie told me it was 'for your own good'. That was nonsense, because I can motivate myself during training. If I want to run, I run; if I don't feel like it, I don't even bother to put on my shoes, or my running feet! It's simple. No amount of shouting will produce a better performance from me.

After the fateful New Year's Eve Van Zijl race in Rand-fontein my training improved a little as the left leg healed – and then the right leg went. Back to the track with the Doctor – this time the Wanderers in Johannesburg on 12 January when I ran 200s. The Doctor tested me after each set of four and, hallelujah, we finally came up with wedges that seemed to work.

On the right track at last, thanks to the Doctor's per-severance, I started getting ready for the English trials to select a team for the world cross-country championships. I couldn't do much apart from slow runs, but at least I was on the move again and I left for Britain in the second week of January, accompanied by the Doctor, who had agreed to be on twenty-four hour alert.

Shortly after our arrival I had a call from Marea Hartman asking me to attend a meeting with her and Mike Farrell at the British Amateur Athletic Board on 21 January. They wanted to know all about the Brakpan incident, which was starting to cause trouble, and I told them truthfully what had happened. They also wanted an assurance that I would stay permanently in Britain. Would I be going to university there? It was obvious the BAAB was under pressure from the Third World members of the IAAF and I told Marea and Mike that I would spend as much time as possible in England, with one proviso: I had to be able to visit South Africa to see the Doctor if the need arose.

As a warm-up for the trials I ran a 5 kilometres race in Oxford on 24 January. The right leg was still sore – muscular pain instead of the deeper-rooted pain that I had experienced previously – but I didn't have too much trouble and I managed to get in a little speed work before the trials six days later.

Brakpan and my relationship with Fanie were all the rage at the trials on 30 January. There were demonstrators everywhere – I couldn't go to the toilet without them following me – and I began to have visions of Liverpool in 1985, when I was forced off the course. To top it all, I ran in spikes that were too short for the slippery conditions and after the first lap I began wondering if I could hold on. 'Keep going,' I told myself. 'You can make the team if you hold on to fourth place.' I wasn't fit enough to make a race of it, but I did cling to fourth place to ensure my selection for England and on 7 February I won a 6.2 mile road race at Epsom in 32:52.

Not bad for a girl with injury problems, but the wedges were starting to work and I found the motivation I needed to train hard, with Christine Kennedy and Mark Davies as willing partners.

163

I was using Fanie's schedules and my reward for my toil was the Doctor's company. It was such fun being with him and he opened my eyes to a whole new world of music, literature and health food, encouraging me to broaden my horizons and look beyond athletics while, at the same time, never losing sight of my goals.

The BAAB called me in again on 1 March and I went to see Marea Hartman and Mike Farrell with John Bryant. The Board wanted further assurances on my South African 'connections' and a lot of detail on how long I had spent out of England. The pressure was building up steadily, with threats of a boycott of the world cross-country championships on 26 April if I took part, and I refused to sign a document specifying the time I had been in South Africa because it could incriminate me. In spite of Fanie's insistence that I train in South Africa, I had not had any choice when I became injured: the only person who could help me was the Doctor – and he lived in South Africa. His treatment had been essential to my recovery and I couldn't let anybody use that as ammunition to shoot me down.

Proof of the success of the Doctor's treatment came in the cross-country at Aldershot on 5 March, when I represented the Women's Cross Country and Road Running Association against Combined Services. I won the 5,360 metres race in 18:00 from Catherine Mijovic; and, with soldiers at the gate, there was no chance of demonstrations. Having two coaches put me in a quandary in this match because although he didn't attend the race, Fanie's advice was 'to take it easy'. John, the man on the spot, urged me to 'run harder' and in the end I ran at my own pace and was well pleased with the result.

My last race before the world cross-country championships was a 5 kilometres event in Belgium on 12 March; in muddy conditions, I finished third, 30 seconds behind Angela Tooby. Back in Guildford that night, I had a call from Les Jones, who told me that there would be 'problems' if I ran in New Zealand. On 14 March the IAAF asked the

BAAB to withdraw me because of the incidents at Brakpan and Randfontein and I was devastated. There had been no problem at two previous championships when I ran against the same countries, so why should things be any different now? I had not done anything wrong . . . I had broken no rules.

In desperation I phoned Fanie, who seemed to be more interested in my 'failure' in Belgium: 'Your mental attitude is all wrong', he said. But what about the fact that the IAAF wanted me out of the world championships: 'No problem,' he said. 'They can't kick you out.'

But it looked as if they would, indeed, ban me and, rather than jeopardize my English teammates, I withdrew from the side on 16 March.

Fanie came to England shortly afterwards and, although I initially looked forward to seeing him, an uneasy atmosphere settled on the house after his arrival. The Doctor loved classical music; Fanie hated it. The solution? When Fanie was downstairs the music centre was turned off, when he was upstairs it was back on. In addition, Fanie could not understand it when the Doctor, who practised Eastern Orthodox religion, fasted. Fanie liked to eat out, so eat out we did, which made life difficult.

Things were different, though, when I had the Doctor to myself. I went to church with him and really enjoyed it, and he would advise me on what clothes to buy. It was the Doctor's turn to look perplexed when he discovered that I was content to walk into one shop, buy whatever caught my eye, and leave it at that. One day I bought some new shoes which I wore to church and my feet were so sore the Doctor said he could see the pain written all over my face. We had to hunt for another, more comfortable, pair and he laughed when I selected flat shoes that would have better suited a nurse.

It was the Doctor who introduced me to opera and literature. Going into a book shop with him was murder, because he would stop every few steps to ask if I had read this book, or was acquainted with the works of that author. He got me to read *Watership Down* (I dreamed about rabbits for weeks afterwards) and encouraged me to write. He showed me that here was a wider view of life and the Doctor's thinking was totally opposed to that of Fanie.

To Fanie money was important; and after my withdrawal from the English world championship team he asked me what my priorities were. I said the Olympic Games in Seoul and he replied that if I was barred from the Olympics I should go to America to make money on the road-running circuit. Again we had a difference of opinion, because I didn't run for money. Sure, money is important and I like having money to buy the things I want, but money alone is not enough motivation to keep me running. I run to grow, to mature as an athlete, and the prospect of racing for $20,000 in big American road races did not hold much appeal for me. In fact road races only appealed to me if they were championships, something of a challenge. Running for money had caused me too much trouble in the past – especially the Decker rematch – and financial reward played no part in the satisfaction I got from competing with distinction in an important and challenging event.

The Doctor could understand my viewpoint about money, but not Fanie and I was forced one night into a situation similar to the one that had existed between Pieter and my father four years previously. At Mark's parents' house for dinner one night – his father, Tom, was away on business, but Mark's mother, Mauchy, was there and his sister Tamara and brother Nick – Fanie stayed out of a conversation that revolved around the arts. He didn't seem to be enjoying the talk and went and sat in the living-room, forcing a division in the gathering. Mark and I joined Fanie who at 10.30 said it was time to go home. The Doctor was, however, testing Nick and Tamara because they too needed wedges in their shoes to correct body imbalances and eventually Fanie said he couldn't wait any longer and

166

left. Although I could have asserted myself and stayed on, I followed Fanie and the Doctor was furious. I had sided with Fanie against the one man who had given me real hope and I felt dreadful.

There was to come a time when the Doctor would accuse me of worrying too much about myself to think about other people and because he was right I felt ashamed. Although they had been friends for years, Fanie thought the Doctor was making me 'soft' by exposing me to the arts. He regarded the Doctor as a bad influence and I suddenly feared that my relationship with Fanie would end in much the same way as my relationship with Pieter and this was heightened by a training session with John Bryant, when Fanie told John he should shout at me 'because she needs it'.

Fanie was, however, still my coach and adviser and we agreed that I would go to America with the Doctor to look at colleges and run a road race. But, again, there was no forward planning and when I asked him what would happen after my return from the US, he said I should stay in Guildford with the Doctor. He did not give a moment's thought to the fact that the Doctor might not be happy in Guildford and I was taken back to the time when Pieter and Carin were with me in England when they would rather have been in South Africa. I started feeling guilty about the Doctor and wondered what would happen.

One of my worst experiences before the IAAF recommended to the BAAB that I be suspended for twelve months occurred when Fanie, the Doctor and I met Mel Batty to talk shoe contracts. I felt like a cow at an auction as they haggled over the price, with Fanie holding out for £10,000 and Mel saying I wasn't worth that much. 'She's been beaten in Belgium by Angela Tooby, and Tooby doesn't get £10,000', said Mel.

On 19 March the Doctor and I left for America and when we got to Cleveland I surprisingly regained my enthusiasm for running. I had a couple of good training sessions there,

167

but I felt as though I had been kicked in the teeth when, as I was on the verge of travelling to New York to run a 10 kilometres race in Central Park on 27 March, an official of the TAC contacted me to break the news that the IAAF had decided on 24 March to suspend me until a council meeting on 15 April when they would consider whether I had broken rule 53(1). They had pinned the Brakpan and Randfontein incidents to me and, not knowing which way to turn, I rang Fanie.

'What should I do?' I asked in desperation. When I heard Fanie's reply, I knew it was all over between us: 'Do anything you like. Why not go to the beach?' I was furious he was so non-committal, and the Doctor and I decided the best thing would be to get back to England as soon as possible; we were in Guildford at the beginning of April.

One last phone call to Fanie didn't produce anything startling and he shocked me when he said the Doctor should move out of the house.

I might have lost Fanie, but I still had John, and once I recovered from a bout of flu I tried to get back into training. But my heart wasn't in it. I knew I had very little chance of beating the IAAF, and I told John that it was time for me to retire. I was tired of the merry-go-round . . . too much had happened. My father, Pieter, Harry and now Fanie. When would it ever stop?

John told me to give myself some time to think and sort things out and he arranged for me to train at Kingston Club, which was kind of him. I even ran a 10-mile race at Richmond Park, finishing sixth in 57:27, but I picked up a lung infection which required antibiotics to knock it out.

On the morning of the IAAF's enquiry on 15 April I got up early and took my dog Basjan out for a walk before spending all day at the Park Lane Hotel. I drank tea, ate biscuits and prowled around, waiting for a decision which the 23-member council was not going to make. It was referred to a five-man inner caucus and that evening John Bryant

168

wanted to drive me home. I declined and asked him to drop me off at Waterloo Station, where I bought a packet of chips and climbed aboard the train, sitting opposite a man who was reading the *Evening Standard*. There was a picture of me in the paper fleeing from the Park Lane Hotel and the man looked at it, looked at me and looked back at the paper. There I was, eating chips and drinking a diet coke in the train and he suddenly realized who I was. 'Oh,' he said, 'it's you! Do you want to read it?' I said no, I didn't read stories about myself, so he very kindly kept the outside pages and gave me the inside to read.

When I got home I told the Doctor I expected to be banned and the next day the news came through. The IAAF had pressurized the BAAB by recommending that I be suspended for twelve months for being in breach of the spirit of the rules of the IAAF. My world had come crashing down. Although the BAAB met on 23 April and decided to investigate my so-called South African connections by forming a committee which was to report back on 21 May, I knew the battle was lost.

I was lucky to have my mother and Quintus with me – Ma arrived on 21 April – because my health was deteriorating. I couldn't sleep and I didn't feel like eating. I was terribly lethargic; my tiredness became like a sickness and I watched TV until the early hours of the morning, wandering around the house wide-eyed when I wasn't sleeping.

On 29 April I went into London to see the BAAB's lawyers and recounted in detail both incidents. After I had signed an affidavit they produced a statement from Fanie which contradicted my evidence and I had no explanation for it. Although he would later sign an affidavit putting both events into perspective, the lawyers suggested I make a public statement dissociating myself from Fanie. I refused for the sake of Corrie, Stephan and Minette and decided against further legal action because I had no income and I could not afford a huge legal bill. I just wanted out.

The situation slowly deteriorated. I didn't train and in an

169

attempt to keep myself occupied I started knitting. The time had come to go back to South Africa because I was losing myself: not only my international career, but everything I felt for athletics. Nobody could understand how precious my running was to me. I didn't just run with my legs, but with my head, and unless I have my love of running to motivate me I am hopeless, anybody can beat me. At the end of April, I was losing that affection for my sport and I was losing interest in everything around me. I had to get away because I couldn't stand getting up every morning with a heavy feeling of despair in my stomach and I was ready to leave in early May.

John Bryant came to see me and we went to the Farmhouse tea-shop where I told him how I felt. He said the best strategy was for me to get booked off for an extended period on medical grounds – which were quite relevant at that stage – and told me that he would speak to Les Jones about it so I could leave as soon as possible.

I saw Victor, my accountant, on 3 May and told him I wanted to quit and I settled down to wait for Les to contact me. When he didn't call I phoned him and he said I had to wait until the BAAB hearing on 21 May; but I couldn't hold on for so long. At that stage an hour was too long and Ma phoned a doctor we knew who came around and examined me. I was on the verge of a breakdown and after a long talk and a thorough examination he agreed to book me off for a year, which would enable me to return to South Africa to recuperate.

The doctor, Ken Kingsbury, later said in an interview that I was 'a pitiful sight, prone to bouts of crying and deep depressions . . . all the clinical signs of anxiety.'

'A breakdown?' he added, 'I prefer the term nervous exhaustion. She could not be allowed to continue like this. She needs her family and her friends; people who will not ask questions, demand decisions.'

The next day John Bryant came around and was initially upset that I had seen the doctor without his knowledge.

'When do you want to leave?' asked John. 'Tonight', I replied. Ma and I had already bought the air tickets, made the arrangements for my animals Sangiro and Basjan to fly to South Africa and put the house on the market. Even if John had objected nothing was going to hold me back.

I told John that although this was the end of a particular kind of relationship, I hoped it would not be the end of our friendship and, when he left, I packed my bags and caught the plane that night, 9 May, leaving Ma and the Doctor to follow a day later.

The statement I issued when I left, said it all:

> Pressure of recent events have told on my health to such an extent that at the moment I no longer feel well enough to continue in competitive athletics. My general medical practitioner and other medical advisers have told me that I am suffering from nervous exhaustion and that I need a substantial period of recuperation along with the support of my family and friends to regain my health.
>
> The doctors further advize that I need a prolonged period away from competition in order to recover fully and that, despite my repeated assurances that I have broken no rules, I am not at the moment well enough to continue the fight to prove my innocence. I am, therefore, on medical advice, withdrawing from international competition during this period of recovery. I hope that the world, the press and the public will respect my need to regain my equilibrium and allow me a period of peaceful recuperation.
>
> I sincerely thank the many people in Great Britain who are supporting me during this crisis and I hope that in the future I will be able to represent them internationally once more.

After my return to Bloemfontein it took several days for it to sink in that I was actually back in the Free State and I hadn't left it a moment too soon. Had I stayed longer I would have lost all my affinity for running and when I looked at myself on television or in the newspaper I saw another person. 'The person everybody is talking about and writing about isn't me,' I told my family. 'That's somebody else.' They didn't understand.

17
Politics is Private

I would, I suppose, have saved myself a great deal of trouble and torment had I taken the easy way out and denounced apartheid from the moment I qualified to run for Britain. But I have never been one to look for a simple solution to a complex problem and because I objected to being a pawn in a political chess game, to being moved around the board at the whim of every anti-apartheid lobbyist who could get a few seconds on television or a couple of paragraphs in a newspaper, I kept my mouth shut and my feelings to myself. I accept that politics is an integral part of daily life but, as a sportswoman, I don't believe that I am in a position to pass judgment on any particular political system. Of course, I have my own views on politics, but because I am not a politician I prefer to keep them to myself. That was not, however, good enough for the opponents of South Africa's policy of racial segregation and even though I was technically British I was also white and born in South Africa, which made me an easy target for anti-apartheid activists around the world.

Sam Ramsamy and his SA Non-Racial Olympic Committee had a field day when I was in England and 'Zola bashing' became a popular sport for the Third World members of the IAAF. I still find it incredible that my opponents thought that by destroying my athletic career they would be striking a major blow against South Africa and the ultimate irony of it all was that I abhor apartheid as they do. But, because people such as Ramsamy and Archbishop Desmond Tutu attacked me as an individual, I refused to accede to their demands.

There were other reasons, too, for the silence I only broke in January 1989, when it became apparent that my reluctance to speak out against apartheid was being misconstrued as support for a political system which deprived the majority of South Africans of their basic human rights. Although I ended up doing political science as part of my BA degree, it had never been my intention to get seriously involved in politics. I chose political science at the suggestion of my coach, Pieter but before that politics had always been something in the distance that other people were involved in.

My political baptism came when I arrived in England and was perceived as a symbol of apartheid. Call me naïve, but at that stage I didn't believe that politics should play a role in the life of an athlete. I still hold that view and it distresses me that politics has become such an overpowering force in the sporting arena. My attitude is that, as a sportswoman, I should have the right to pursue my chosen discipline in peace. Wendy Sly isn't asked if she voted Labour or Conservative; Seb Coe does not get asked to denounce Soviet expansionism; and Carl Lewis is not required to express his view on the Contra arms scandal. But I was not afforded that courtesy, and it became a matter of principle for me not to give those who were intent on discrediting me the satisfaction of hearing me say what they most wanted to hear.

But that was not the only reason why I remained silent. Only a fool speaks publicly on a subject they know very little about and in my late teens I was certainly no expert on political systems. My life revolved around my running

174

and, although I had formed an opinion about what the black, coloured and Asian people in South Africa were being subjected to, I didn't have a firm grasp of the social issues of the day or what was happening in international relations. I had not studied apartheid in any great detail and was not, therefore, in a position to comment when everybody was baying for a statement.

As I matured, I became more cynical about politics and politicians. I looked long and hard, but saw nothing noble in politics and I felt particularly aggrieved by attacks on me by people who imputed that I was a racist or that I supported a racist political system because I did not make a stand against apartheid. I saw no reason why, for the sake of expediency, I should sacrifice my belief in honesty and fair play. There was certainly nothing fair about the way anti-apartheid activists picked on me – even Archbishop Tutu indicated that I was a legitimate target in the bid to isolate South Africa – and apart from wanting to stay clear of the political circus in the first place, I felt sure I would not be left alone once I had stated my opposition to apartheid. My fear was that once I denounced apartheid I would be asked to condemn the South African government, the State President, or the tricameral parliament in a never ending spiral.

Even people connected closely with me, staunch South Africans, wanted me to come out against apartheid and I was in a no-win situation. I didn't want to antagonize anyone and even though I can never accept a political system which entrenches the superiority of one race or culture over another, my thoughts on the subject were my affair. In 1986 I came under a lot of pressure from Pieter to put my pride in my pocket and speak out against apartheid. Jannie Momberg, too, wanted me to clear the air and former Springbok cricketer Eddie Barlow, then based in London as South Africa's sporting 'ambassador', even prepared a statement for me. Had I endorsed the document, dated 7 July 1986, this is what I would have said:

175

I should make it quite clear that I am now a British citizen, proud to be so, and indebted to the British people for the warmth and friendship they have shown towards me.

I am aware that my South African background has given rise to much comment. As a former South African athlete, I fully supported the policy of the South African sporting community which unequivocally rejected apartheid and called for its abolition.

Now that I have become a British citizen my views are unchanged, and I remain wholly opposed not only to apartheid, but to any form of discrimination practised anywhere in the world on any grounds. I am sure that my concern with violations of human rights is the same as that felt by all my fellow sportsmen and women.

I am sure a statement such as that would have done much to defuse the explosive situation in which I found myself in England, yet I was not prepared to compromise my original belief in the fact that an individual's political views were personal. I agreed with every word, but I was a runner, not a politician, and if other sportsmen and women were not required to make similar statements, I did not see why I should be the exception. The more I was pressed into taking a stand the more I rebelled; Pieter used to get angry every time the subject came up and I routinely refused to speak my mind. In the end my determination not to give in played right into my opponents' hands by giving them still more ammunition to fire back at me. But my conscience was clear, and that was the main thing.

Not surprisingly, there was hardly a murmur when, on 3 January 1989, I made what was, at the time, the most explicit political statement of my career, after being labelled a supporter of apartheid through the distortion of my words in a television interview and in a documentary made by British film-maker Kenneth Griffith. In the interview I reiterated that I would never condemn apartheid and in the other I criticized Archbishop Tutu and Sam Ramsamy for attacking me personally. That I had dared point a finger at Archbishop Tutu, one of the South African government's fiercest critics, rekindled the controversy surrounding my own political stance, and I had to 'go public' for the first time to rid myself of the pro-apartheid image I had gained through my criticism.

Still hesitant to commit myself, I argued that by questioning the tactics of Archbishop Tutu and Mr Ramsamy I was not supporting a political system which deprived many South Africans of their basic human rights. My quarrel with them was not over apartheid, but over the way they had attacked me and I did not believe they had any right to use me as a target in their bid to dismantle apartheid. I continued in a statement released through the South African Press Association:

> As an athlete who still hopes to pursue an international career I am not interested in joining the political circus and I have always resisted attempts to force me into taking a particular political stance. I object to being used as a political pawn and as a matter of principle do not think that my own political views, or those of any sportsman or woman, should be a matter for public concern. An athlete, however, does not have to be a politician to recognize that people everywhere have basic human rights and I, as a Christian, hold that view. I do not support any political system that entrenches the superiority of one race over another.

Several days later, in an interview with Johannesburg newspaper *Sunday Star*, I went further, saying that 'even the State President, Mr P.W. Botha, has rejected apartheid and I hold the same view.'

Although I had finally shown my colours, there was no reaction from the anti-apartheid lobby and the reason was simple. It suited them when I kept quiet, but my personal politics were of no use to them if I agreed with their point of view. Instead, the African bloc countries in the IAAF changed tack and concentrated on my South African links in an attempt to prevent a Budd comeback and I was left wondering why I had bothered in the first place. It had to be said, though, because I couldn't bear the thought of being seen as endorsing apartheid.

You only have to study the Bible to recognize the injustice of apartheid. The Bible tells me that all men are born equal and that we will all be equal before God. I cannot reconcile segregation along racial lines with the teaching of the Bible, and as a Christian I find apartheid intolerable. I do not support apartheid and I took exception to the people who, when I was silent on the issue, used me as a means of scoring political points. Archbishop Tutu was among the many who singled me out for attack, endorsing the call for action to be taken against me because of my South African links, yet he didn't for one moment consider that I might share his view that apartheid should be dismantled. Instead, he called on athletics administrators to take whatever steps were necessary to ensure that my international career was brought to an abrupt end and I don't understand how my absence from the 1988 Olympic Games struck a blow against South Africa.

Sam Ramsamy embarked on frequent 'Hammer Zola' sprees in the British media. It amuses me to think that when I left England in 1988 on medical advice to recuperate after the trauma of the IAAF's investigation into my South African 'links', Mr Ramsamy had to look elsewhere for drums on which to beat his anti-apartheid rhythm.

178

This was his parting shot, published in *The Times* of 11 May: 'She has been such a nuisance. But I think we have now seen the back of her; I doubt if she will return here to run. If she had made a strong statement against apartheid and genuinely cut her links with South Africa, we would have accepted her, but she did neither.'

My statement of 3 January 1989, explained why I did neither earlier in my career and if Mr Ramsamy considered me a nuisance, he was generally harmless as far as I was concerned and I seldom became annoyed over his outbursts. Luckily for me, the men and women in the street in Britain were very positive whenever I came into contact with them and while the politicians ranted on and on about my 'passport of convenience', the general public made me very welcome.

It's odd how the attitude expressed by politicians often differs from that of the people they represent and the same paradox exists in South Africa. The big difference here is that the people who greet me in the street have no power base at all because they are black. If the anti-apartheid lobby was to be believed, you would expect blacks to give me the cold shoulder, yet many of the people who actually make an attempt to speak to me instead of standing and pointing are black. I grew up on a farm with a black boy, Thipe, who became my best friend and if my family went visiting and I 'disappeared', I was often found in the kitchen talking to the black domestic workers. In my own experience, black people are more sincere than whites – I have never been hurt emotionally by a black person – and I can understand and sympathize with their frustration in not having a say in how the country in which they live is governed. I don't have the answer to the many problems in South Africa that revolve around the colour of a man's skin, but I do know that the basis of the solution is common sense and compromise.

179

18
Love and Marriage

The best thing to come out of the sordid mess surrounding my twelve month suspension was meeting Mike Pieterse again. Mike is a member of a prominent Bloemfontein family, and I met him casually in 1986 through my sister Estelle and one of my friends, Marinda Botha, who used to work for him at the liquor outlet he owns in partnership with his brother Theoneil. But I never dreamed then that we would end up getting engaged. And who would have guessed that someone supposedly as shy as poor little Zola would be the one to pop the question?

When I was running internationally I never had time to think about men, because my lifestyle was too unsettled. Flitting between South Africa, England, Europe and America made it impossible for me to form relationships at any level anywhere and I had also taken such an emotional pounding from the very people who were meant to be looking after me that I found it difficult to form any close attachments. Once bitten, twice shy, and the last thing I needed was to become romantically and emotionally involved with somebody who might let me down. With Mike, though, it was different.

'I'll never marry,' I once told Dr Holder. 'Oh yes you will,' he replied, in what was to become a standing joke between us. 'If the chemicals are there they are there and you will not be able to do anything about it.' There had, of course, been other boyfriends, but none of the relationships ever looked like turning into something serious. Meeting Mike again resulted in a whirlwind courtship that took us both by surprise. Dr Holder's joke about chemicals became reality because there was an immediate reaction when we were together. I knew we had something special going for us after we went to the Thaba Nchu Sun hotel with three friends to play video games and have dinner. That's when we really started getting acquainted: finding out about each other, laughing and joking. We got together again to watch videos at my mother's house and the next day we had a braaivleis (barbecue) together. Everything started falling into place and I knew my life was about to change.

At a time when I was feeling very unsure of myself after being sacrificed by the IAAF as they pandered to their Third World members, I suddenly found this lovely man – my big cuddly teddy bear is how one press report described him – and it was virtually love at first sight. I'd had my eye on Mike before the evening at Thaba Nchu Sun (although it is a casino neither of us gambled) and with the assistance of my family, I had great fun in plotting his capture. When I was ill in bed I asked Estelle to get Mike to visit me and when my piano arrived from England I phoned Mike and asked him to come and see it. I wanted somebody special to be there for one of my special moments. Mike was that somebody.

Within a month I knew Mike was the sort of man a girl dreams about – solid, dependable, loving and a lot of fun. We did not even talk about athletics and the relationship developed so fast that I knew I had to do something.

What I did took everyone except Mike by surprise. We had fallen in love, but I couldn't stand the thought of being hurt again. I wasn't prepared to give any more of

myself emotionally in the relationship without more security, only to find out after a few months that it was just a
casual friendship, so I took the initiative. 'Listen Mike,' I
said to him one day in August when he was visiting me at
the townhouse I was renting. 'If you want this relationship
to grow and become stronger I have got to have a commitment from you. Let's get married?'

There, I had done it and it wasn't half as difficult as I
thought it would be! I don't even think Mike was particularly surprised because he must have seen it coming. He
agreed immediately and we initially decided to make the
announcement at the end of September.

I was so relieved to know that my love for Mike was
reciprocated, but still we kept our engagement a secret.
We only 'went public' when my mother had to go into
hospital for an operation. She was very depressed and
because we wanted to cheer her up, to spur her on, we
decided to break the news to her first. Mike came round
one day and said, 'Let's go and buy a ring', and we left on
what was to be the fastest shopping expedition you could
imagine.

I know it sounds silly, but we felt like a couple of embarrassed kids when we went to the jewellery shop. Obviously,
I am well known in Bloemfontein, as are the members of the
Pieterse family, so we parked Mike's bakkie (truck) about
three blocks from Gerrards Jewellers in Bloemfontein's main
street and sneaked in; we had agreed to get out as fast as
possible. Everybody's eyes were bulging when they saw us
looking at rings. We made our choice within five minutes,
but had to leave the ring at the shop because it was too big
and Mike didn't even get a chance to put it on my finger
himself. When I went back to the shop to pick up the ring
the lady asked me what I wanted her to do. 'Shall I put it
into a box for you?' she asked. 'No,' I replied. 'Just put it
on my finger.'

Once we had the ring we had to show my mother, who
was already in hospital. It was 24 August and I hung around

during visiting hours because I was still embarrassed. When all the others had left, I showed Ma and dashed outside to join Mike. I didn't even wait to see what Ma said, but I knew she would be delighted because she had always liked Mike; she rang us both later that evening.

Everyone was happy for us, though my sisters and brother were quite shocked. I think Ma knew Mike and I were very close and she must have realized that something was up when I stopped fighting with her. As always, the only member of the family who couldn't join in the celebrations was my father. After all that happened in making me 'British' and the trauma of the build-up to the Olympics, I still have had very little to do with him, although I did ring him after the engagement to tell him. He was pleased for me.

What a different person I was at the time of the engagement from the girl who, a few months earlier, had been on the verge of a mental breakdown – wandering wide-eyed around the house in Guildford with a pillow under my arm because I couldn't sleep. Now, the crying sessions and agonizing waiting while the hypocrites at the IAAF decided my fate were all behind me. For the first time in four years my life was 'normal'. I had my man, I was at university studying political science and ethnology and I was back in training.

Once we were engaged, we didn't waste any time before tying the knot. The wedding was set for 15 April 1989 and I was really looking forward to it. I know that a bride's wedding day is supposed to be the biggest day of her life, but I deliberately kept mine low key. I didn't want it to turn into a society occasion and the guest list was small and select – just family and close friends, with a limited contingent from the media who were there by invitation only.

In normal circumstances, my father would have given me away but, knowing his opposition to the ceremony in a church in which the wedding march was not played, I

183

couldn't ask him. I had, of course, planned to invite my father, but I wanted my brother, Quintus, to give me away and that's when the trouble started. My father was not happy with that arrangement, going so far as to threaten to disinherit Quintus if he walked me down the aisle. Quintus was quite prepared to incur his father's wrath by giving me away, but he had built his house on property owned by my father and because I didn't want to cause another rift in the family, I asked Mike's father to do the honours instead.

I can only speculate that my father's opposition to Quintus giving me away was prompted by a mistaken belief that I wasn't going to invite him to the wedding. But that just wasn't true. Even though we had had our differences in the past, my father's name was still on the guest list and the only reason he hadn't received his invitation was because I hadn't yet sent them all out. I was, as is so often the case in my private life, running late, but when I heard from other members of my family that my father was talking about disinheriting Quintus over the issue of giving me away, I changed my mind about inviting him.

It was an unfortunate incident and one I wish could have been amicably resolved. Instead, my father said some hurtful things about me to a reporter from the *Sunday Times* newspaper, who splashed it all over the front page the day after the wedding in a story which caused great distress to other members of my family.

I was, however, determined not to let my father's antagonism spoil my big day, which dawned with clouds heavy with rain hanging low in the sky. Rain on your wedding day means good luck, and I needed plenty of that because I was so nervous. It's difficult to explain why I wanted to get the ceremony over and done with, but I think we both wanted to get the formalities over with as quickly as possible so we could get on with our lives. I was more nervous before the wedding than I was before any race and, in a way, it was worse getting married than it was running in the 1984

Olympic Games. When we stood in front of the minister I began trembling so much that Mike had to hold my hand and the rest of the day passed in a blur. I was relieved when it was all over and the best thing was not having to go back to an empty house that night. Mike was with me now to share my life and had I known what contentment marriage would bring, I would have married earlier.

I know that I'm going to be happy with Mike, who will support me all the way, no matter what decisions I make about my athletics career. He was there for me when I tackled the thorny problem of whether to make one last attempt at competing internationally and we were in complete agreement when I decided to call it quits and stay in Bloemfontein.

That announcement was made at a press conference in Johannesburg on 7 June 1989 in the following statement:

> After careful consideration of all the elements affecting my personal and professional life, I have decided not to return to the United Kingdom to pursue my running career.
>
> While I value my British heritage and the opportunity it afforded me to compete internationally, I do not feel that I can comfortably return to England without some regular and open contact with the native soil of the land of my birth.
>
> I wish to thank all the British people who gave me their support.
>
> For those who fought against my participation in international athletics, I harbour no ill will.
>
> I love running and hope to return to competition soon. I have taken control of my own life, however, and in the future will seek to run on my own terms in accordance with factors which do not conflict with my personal beliefs or convictions, and which fit my personal goals and ambitions.

In the end, it wasn't a difficult choice and a poem by W.B. Yeats captures some of the sentiment behind my decision:

THE CHOICE

The intellect of man is forced to choose
Perfection of the life, or of the work,
And if it take the second must refuse

When all that story's finished, what's the news?
In luck or out the toil has left its mark:
That old perplexity an empty purse,
Or the day's vanity, the night's remorse.

For me, life should not revolve around material possessions. We must live life to the full, enjoying every moment, and in making my decision I had to consider the price I would pay if I wanted to get back into the top echelon of international athletics. As a married woman, I just do not have the motivation necessary to make a comeback in the overseas arena. That takes a great deal of dedication and it would be difficult to motivate myself for serious competition. I no longer have an overwhelming urge to beat people, to be the best. I'm not afraid of the competition, I just don't need it any more. I am enjoying life as it is – quietly and without the pressure of a hectic training and racing schedule. I run now because I love it; I can never give it up, but the difference is between running for enjoyment and fulfilment and running for achievement at top level. The difficult years overseas have altered my approach to my sport and if South Africa were to be readmitted to world athletics tomorrow, I don't think I would take part.

I have had enough of competitive athletics. I came to a point in my life where I had to make a decision, because for me to run well I have to work very hard indeed. Not just physically, but mentally. I don't race as much with my legs as with my head and that's why some of my performances were so erratic. I have to gear myself up mentally to do well, and that was difficult while I was competing overseas and had so many other things on my mind apart from the job in hand. I need to be one hundred per cent ready mentally if I am to perform well and that requires a lot of commitment and effort; a commitment I feel I can no longer make now that I am happily married.

In the early days, when I was escaping from the death of my sister, Jenny, running helped me to boost my self-esteem. I always felt inferior to other people when I was younger – my personality being such that I found it difficult to communicate with people. It took me a long time to trust people (it still does) and by running well I was able to show people just what I was capable of. It almost became an obsession to gain the respect of those around me through my performance on the track. I got a kick out of doing well and I felt proud of myself after a particularly good run. It wasn't something I showed to the world, but I felt it inside, in my heart, where it counts. Perhaps the most important decision of all was the one which allowed me to accept myself for what I am. I am content as Zola Pieterse and the choice I had to make was not as straightforward as it appeared on the outside. It wasn't as simple as running in South Africa or running overseas, but rather a choice between running and life. I chose life.

Like every woman, I want to have children, but that will be later, rather than sooner. I used to be afraid of babies because they are so small, but since I became an aunt I have learned to cope with them. Before I start thinking of raising a family, though, I have some running to do. And if any of my children inherit some of my genes and show a talent for athletics, I will never push them the way I was pushed into the international spotlight. If children of mine want to run it must be because they love the sport, because they enjoy competition and because of the challenge. That's how it was for me until that fateful day in January 1984, when my unofficial world 5,000 metres record at Stellenbosch turned a shy young Afrikaans girl into a commodity; a money-making machine who was expected to reel out a continuous string of world class performances, no matter how homesick she was, or how much she hated being away from her beloved South Africa.

The Zola Budd who competed overseas from 1984 to 1987 was really two different people, the one you saw on television and in the newspapers, and me as I really am. The Zola everybody thinks they know, the public Zola, is dead: she has been buried and only the real Zola remains. I may still run again, but if I do it will be on my terms. I will never again allow myself to be used and abused to bring fame and fortune to other people.

Milestones

Races in Zola Budd's career

(The races for each year are given chronologically, with track races being followed by road and cross-country events)

DATE	DISTANCE	TIME	PLACE	VENUE	NOTES
1980					
Track					
19/09	3,000m	10:19.8	(4)	Bloemfontein	S. Cronje 9:32.9
08/10	1,500m	4:32.00	(1)	Bloemfontein	
08/10	800m	2:16.5	(1)	Bloemfontein	
13/10	3,000m	10:06.5	(3)	Bloemfontein	S. Gerber 9:59.9
13/10	800m	2:17.3	(2)	Bloemfontein	S. Gerber 2:14.5
28/10	1,500m	4:27.8	(1)	Bloemfontein	
28/10	800m	2:17.4	(1)	Bloemfontein	
12/11	1,500m	4:24.3	(2)	Bloemfontein	S. Gerber 4:20.4
12/11	800m	2:19.5	(5)	Bloemfontein	Ilze de Kock 2:07.6
Cross-country					
19/07		14:36	(1)	Bloemfontein	SA Schools
09/08		14:26	(1)	Bloemfontein	OFS u.14 Ch
30/08		16:22	(12)	Pretoria	SA u.14 Ch, C. Bornman 15:30.

DATE	DISTANCE	TIME	PLACE	VENUE	NOTES
1981					
Track					
14/02	1,500m	4:38.2	(3)	Bloemfontein	Cronje 4:14.5
20/02	1,500m	4:20.7	(1)	Bloemfontein	OFS u.16 rec
03/03	1,500m	4:21.7	(1)	Bloemfontein	
03/03	800m	2:13.9	(1)	Bloemfontein	
07/03	800m	2:10.1	(1)	Sasolburg	
27/03	800m	2:10.9	(1)	Sasolburg	
28/03	1,500m	4:29.1	(1)	Sasolburg	
03/04	1,500m	4:22.9	(2)	Bloemfontein	SA u.16 Ch, S. Gerber 4:22.00
04/04	800m	2:15.33	(1h)	Bloemfontein	SA u.16 Ch
04/04	800m	2:11.9	(1)	Bloemfontein	SA u.16 Ch
30/10	800m	2:07.4	(1)	Bloemfontein	
31/10	1,500m	4:19.8	(1)	Bloemfontein	
14/11	1,500m	4:19	(2)	Bloemfontein	S. Gerber 4:18.8
Road					
01/08	10km	34:22	(1)	Bloemfontein	OFS Ch
26/09	10km	35:18	(2)	Cape Town	SA Ch, D. Massyn 34:45
12/12	10km	38:13	(1)	Bethlehem	
31/12	4km	18:33	(1)	Bloemfontein	
Cross-country					
06/06		15:16	(1)	Potchefstroom	
08/08		14:08	(1)	Bloemfontein	OFS Ch
05/09		16:28	(1)	Cape Town	SA u.16 Ch
19/09		13:17	(3)	Pietersburg	SA Pres, D. Massyn 13:02
1982					
Track					
25/01	3,000m	9:07	(1)	Bloemfontein	
08/02	3,000m	9:06.1	(1)	Bloemfontein	

DATE	DISTANCE	TIME	PLACE	VENUE	NOTES
19/02	1,500m	4:09.1	(1)	Bloemfontein	SA u.16 & u.19 rec
06/03	800m	2:06.5	(1)	Sasolburg	SA u.16 rec
06/03	1,500m	4:16.1	(1)	Sasolburg	
12/03	1,500m	4:12.4	(1)	Bloemfontein	
13/03	3,000m	9:14.5	(1)	Bloemfontein	
18/03	1,500m	4:10.1	(1)	Cape Town	
26/03	800m	2:08.20	(1)	Sasolburg	
27/03	1,500m	4:20.05	(1)	Sasolburg	
02/04	3,000m	9:05.70	(1)	Pretoria	SA u.19 Ch; SA u.19 rec
03/04	1,500m	4:15.74	(1)	Pretoria	SA u.19 Ch
16/04	1,500m	4:12.38	(1)	Stellenbosch	SA Ch
17/04	3,000m	8:59.2	(1)	Stellenbosch	SA Ch
23/04	1,500m	4:22.7	(1)	Germiston	
30/04	1,500m	4:21	(1)	Germiston	
03/05	3,000m	9:16.8	(1)	Port Elizabeth	
09/10	3,000m	9:19.5	(1)	Cradock	
16/10	1,500m	4:17.9	(1)	Bloemfontein	
16/10	3,000m	9:13.3	(1)	Bloemfontein	
20/10	1,500m	4:22.22	(1)	Port Elizabeth	
25/10	1,500m	4:15.10	(1)	Stellenbosch	
29/10	3,000m	9:03.5	(1)	Bloemfontein	SA u.19 rec
10/11	1,500m	4:12.1	(1)	Bloemfontein	

Road

DATE	DISTANCE	TIME	PLACE	VENUE	NOTES
20/06	16km	58:59	(1)	Welkom	
31/07	10km	33:36	(1)	Bloemfontein	OFS Ch; SA rec
25/09	10km	34:20	(1)	Bloemfontein	SA Ch
11/12	10km	35:24	(1)	Bethlehem	
31/12	5km	16:18	(1)	Bloemfontein	

Cross-country

DATE	DISTANCE	TIME	PLACE	VENUE	NOTES
04/09		13:56	(1)	Alberton	SA u.16 Ch

DATE	DISTANCE	TIME	PLACE	VENUE	NOTES
1983					
Track					
26/01	3,000m	9:14.8	(1)	Bloemfontein	
29/01	5,000m	15:35.67	(1)	Durban	W jr rec
31/01	3,000m	9:08.9	(1)	Bloemfontein	
07/02	800m	2:06.1+		Bloemfontein	
07/02	1,000m	2:37.9	(2)	Bloemfontein	I. Venter 2:37.2
14/02	3,000m	8:56.8	(1)	Bloemfontein	
18/02	1,500m	4:09.11	(1)	Bloemfontein	
22/02	3,000m	8:46.41	(1)	Stellenbosch	W jr rec
12/03	800m	2:05.04	(1)	Bloemfontein	
12/03	3,000m	9:38.4	(1)	Bloemfontein	
16/03	1,500m	4:17.2	(1)	Pretoria	
16/03	3,000m	9:22.7	(1)	Pretoria	
25/03	800m	2:07.08	(1)	Sasolburg	
26/03	1,500m	4:08.97	(1)	Sasolburg	SA u.19 rec
02/04	3,000m	8:39.00	(1)	Durban	SA u. 19 Ch; W jr rec & SA rec
04/04	1,500m	4:25.32	(1h)	Durban	SA u.19 Ch
04/04	1,500m	4:09.65	(1)	Durban	SA u.19 Ch
15/04	1,500m	4:10.13	(1)	Bloemfontein	SA Ch
16/04	3,000m	9:05.86	(1)	Bloemfontein	SA Ch
19/04	1,500m	4:15.62	(1)	Germiston	
23/04	1,500m	4:17.75	(1)	Sasolburg	
25/04	5,000m	15:24.08	(1)	Stellenbosch	W jr rec
10/10	1,500m	4:23.1	(1)	Bloemfontein	
17/10	5,000m	15:10.65	(1)	Port Elizabeth	W jr rec & SA rec
24/10	5,000m	15:38.75	(1)	Bloemfontein	
28/10	1,500m	4:06.87	(1)	Bloemfontein	SA rec
Road					
18/06	16km	56.43	(1)	Welkom	SA rec
30/07	16km	55:28	(1)	Kathu	SA rec
06/08	10km	32:20	(1)	Bloemfontein	SA rec

192

DATE	DISTANCE	TIME	PLACE	VENUE	NOTES
10/09	10km	34:15	(1)	Bloemfontein	
24/09	10km	32:23	(1)	Bloemfontein	SA Ch
04/10	10km	33:17	(1)	Bloemfontein	
19/10	5.5km	19:15	(1)	Bloemfontein	
31/12	5km	16:02	(1)	Bloemfontein	

Cross-country

DATE	DISTANCE	TIME	PLACE	VENUE	NOTES
21/05		13:26	(1)	Bloemfontein	
13/08		12:56	(1)	Bloemfontein	OFS Ch
03/09		13:14	(1)	Durban	SA Ch
17/09		11:53	(1)	Middelburg	SA Press

1984

Track

DATE	DISTANCE	TIME	PLACE	VENUE	NOTES
05/01	5,000m	15:01.83	(1)	Stellenbosch	W best, W jr rec, SA rec
25/01	3,000m	9:07.42	(1)	Potchefstroom	
30/01	mile	4:37.52	(1)	Bloemfontein	
06/02	2,000m	5:44.4	(1)	Bloemfontein	W jr rec & SA rec
15/02	3,000m	9:03.8	(1)	Stellenbosch	
20/02	1,500m	4:05.81	(1)	Bloemfontein	W jr rec & SA rec
25/02	3,000m	9:05.9	(1)	Pretoria	
29/02	3,000m	8:37.5	(1)	Stellenbosch	W jr rec & SA rec
05/03	3,000m	8:52.84	(1)	Germiston	
07/03	5,000m	15:09.86	(1)	Port Elizabeth	
16/03	800m	2:00.9	(1)	Kroonstad	
21/03	1,500m	4:01.81	(1)	Port Elizabeth	W jr rec & SA rec
21/03	3,000m	8:54.7	(1)	Port Elizabeth	
14/04	3,000m	9:02.6	(1)	Dartford	UK jr rec
25/04	1,500m	4:10.82	(1)	London	
27/05	1,500m	4:16.27	(1h)	Cwmbran	UK Ch
28/05	1,500m	4:04.39	(1)	Cwmbran	UK Ch; Eur jr rec
06/06	3,000m	8:40.22	(1)	London	OT; Eur jr rec
19/06	3,000m	8:51.99	(1)	Belfast	

DATE	DISTANCE	TIME	PLACE	VENUE	NOTES
23/06	1,500m	4:14.22	(1)	Birmingham	
13/07	mile	4:30.7+	(1)	London	W jr rec
13/07	2,000m	5:33.15	(1)	London	W jr rec & W rec
08/08	3,000m	8:44.62	(3h)	Los Angeles	OG, M. Puica 8:43.32
10/08	3,000m	8:48.80	(7)	Los Angeles	OG, M. Puica 8:35.96

Road

06/05	10km	31:42	(3)	Oslo	I. Kristiansen 31:25
30/12	8km	26:27	(1)	Zurich	

1985

Track

29/06	3,000m	8:44.54	(1)	Gateshead	vs France, CSSR
04/07	5,000m	15:13.07	(6)	Helsinki	WG, M. Puica 15:06.04
20/07	3,000m	8:45.43	(4)	London	PTG, M. Slaney 8:32.91
23/07	mile	4:23.14	(1)	Edinburgh	
09/08	1,500m	4:03.36+		Gateshead	
09/08	mile	4:22.96	(1)	Gateshead	
17/08	3,000m	8:35.32	(1)	Moscow	EC; UK rec
21/08	1,500m	4:00.79+		Zurich	WK
21/08	mile	4:17.57	(3)	Zurich	WK; Com rec, M. Slaney 4:16.71
26/08	5,000m	14:48.07	(1)	London	W rec
30/08	1,500m	3:59.96	(3)	Brussels	Van D; Com rec, M. Slaney 3:57.2
07/09	2,000m	5:39.2+		Rome	GP
07/09	3,000m	8:28.83	(3)	Rome	GP; Com rec, M. Slaney 8:25.83

Road

02/03	10km	32:20	(2)	Phoenix	W. Sly 32:03
24/11	10km	32:29	(1)	Rosemont	
01/12	10km	33:15	(1)	San Diego	

DATE	DISTANCE	TIME	PLACE	VENUE	NOTES

Cross-country

16/02				Liverpool	UK Ch. Demonstrators prevented Zola finishing.
24/03		15:01	(1)	Lisbon	W Ch; 5km

1986

Track

25/01	1,500m	4:06.87i	(1)	Cosford	UK Ch
08/02	3,000m	8:39.79i	(1)	Cosford	W rec
07/06	1,500m	4:01.93	(1)	Birmingham	WAAA Ch
30/06	3,000m	8:34.43	(1)	Belfast	UG
11/07	mile	4:27.5+		London	PTG
11/07	2,000m	5:30.19	(3)	London	PTG, M. Puica 5:28.69
13/08	3,000m	8:45.76	(3)	Zurich	WK, I. Kristiansen 8:34.10
28/08	3,000m	8:38.20	(4)	Stuttgart	Eur Ch, O. Bondarenko
31/08	1,500m	4:05.32	(9)	Stuttgart	Eur Ch, R. Agletdinova 4:01.19

Cross-country

23/03		14:50	(1)	Neuchâtel	W Ch; 4.65km

1987

Road

04/09	5km	16:14	(-)	Hyde Park	
13/09	2 miles	10:24	(1)	Horsham	
19/09	10km	32:17	(1)	Bangor	KC
04/10	3km	8:54	(1)	Biella	
15/11	6 miles	32:56	(1)	Portsmouth	

DATE	DISTANCE	TIME	PLACE	VENUE	NOTES

1988

Road

| 07/01 | 6.2 miles | 32:52 | (1) | Epsom | |

Cross-country

| 30/01 | | 18:42 | (4) | Gateshead | WCCT; 5.4km, A. Tooby 18:06 |
| 05/03 | | 18:00 | (1) | Aldershot | vs Combined Services |

Abbreviations and notes

Ch	Championships
Com	Commonwealth
EC	European Cup
Eur	European
GP	Grand Prix
h	heat
ha	handicap
i	indoor
jr	junior
KC	Kodak Classic
OFS	Orange Free State
OG	Olympic Games
OT	Olympic Trials
Pres	Prestige meeting
PTG	Peugeot Talbot Games
rec	record
UG	Ulster Games
UK	United Kingdom
Van D	Van Damme meeting
W	World
WAAA	Women's AAA Championships
WCCT	World cross-country trials
WG	World Games
WK	Weltklasse meeting
+	intermediate time in longer race

Zola Budd's career statistics were supplied by Riël Hauman.

Index

199